DATE DUE

SEP 18 '97			
FE 6 '98			
JE 11 '98			
JY 9 '98			
SE 23 '98			
AU 0 '04			
JA 15 '07			
MR 1 0 '11			
AP 0 9			
FE 1 0 '14			

DEDICATION

To Lili Hyatt, my beloved wife and partner for 22 years-
for her constant love and steadfast encouragement,
unerringly wise counsel and unfailing support in
my researching and writing this book from the
moment of my first thought of doing it a decade ago.

To John White, author and literary agent, for his faith
in my book and for his persistent search to find
the "right" publisher and the "right" home
for this book.

To George W. Fisk, author, minister, and metaphysical
book publisher, for enthusiastically welcoming
this book to his publishing house, and for
his many creative editorial suggestions.

Above all others this book owes its existence to these
three special, gifted, wonderful people. Without their
magnificent help, it would never have been published.

D. H.

YOUR LIFE

AND LOVE

BEYOND DEATH

DAVID HYATT

Cosmic Concepts
2531 Dover Lane
St. Joseph, Michigan 49085

YOUR LIFE AND LOVE BEYOND DEATH

© by David Hyatt, 1992

Library of Congress Cataloging-in-Publication Data

Hyatt, Dave.
        Your life and love beyond death / David Hyatt.
                p. cm.
        Includes bibliographical references.
        ISBN 0-9620507-3-3 : $11.95
        1. Spiritualism--Case studies. 2. Future life-Case studies.
3. Near-death experiences. I. Title.
BF1261.2.H93   1992   92-27748
133.9--dc20   CIP

printed and bound in the United States of America

10 9 8 7 6 5 4 3 2 1

published by
COSMIC CONCEPTS Press
2531 Dover Lane, St. Joseph, MI 49085

FOREWORD

With *Your Life and Love Beyond Death*, David Hyatt has not only written a powerful book about a fascinating subject which is of compelling interest to everyone (whether we are consciously aware of it or not), but he provides us with a testament of faith and hope which inspires us and lifts us to higher levels of consciousness and awareness.

Your Life and Love Beyond Death occupies a priority position in my life which is already filled with many books which I have written and thousands more I have read and studied. Since I first received the work in manuscript from the author, it has been one of my most valued possessions, as I know it will be yours.

The author has skillfully mixed the familiar with the new, within a unique framework of thorough research, faultless scholarship, and spiritual inspiration projected by his personal revelations and experiences, and his all-embracing love for humankind, as evidenced by his many years of service as an active worker and eventual president of the National Conference of Christians and Jews. The love which David Hyatt has for life and all living things throbs from every page of this precious testament to the wonder, sacredness, and eternity of all life.

As if this were not enough, David Hyatt writes with a clarity, simplicity and power of style which reveals to you dimensions of meaning which transcend the printed page. His explanations, and interpretations of Universal principles are only transcended by the lessons and revelations which have come to him through his own experiences, and which he now shares so generously and lovingly with everyone.

It is my fervent prayer that this dedicated book, written with such care and compassion and deep love for all humankind, may be read by every person who is seeking the meaning of life, and by those who will be led to this seeking by the reading.

May you read *Your Life and Love Beyond Death* many times for inspiration, reassurance and knowledge, as I have done, and may you then share the book and its concepts with many others, helping them also to more fully realize that Life is a glorious adventure that never ends!

- DONALD CURTIS, D.D.
Minister, Unity Church of Dallas
Author of *Your Thoughts Can Change Your Life,*
Human Problems and How to Solve Them,
New Age Understanding,
The Way of the Christ,
and many other books.

CONTENTS

We now have evidence that
death is simply graduation
from earthly life
to a more beautiful life
on a higher plane!

There is no death!

I am writing this book so that those who have lost a dear one - whether husband or wife, or father or mother, or son or daughter, or brother or sister, or close relative or beloved friend - will be reassured that they still live on.

Actually there is no death. There is only life - vibrant, beautiful - beyond the so-called "death" we earthlings experience.

The human race since the dawn of history has in some vague way always believed this, has always held a faith in some sort of life beyond death - a happy hunting ground, a nirvana, a heaven, and even a return to earth in reincarnation. All of the world's great religions proclaim "there is no death!" But they offer no proof.

Today, however, we have a mass of evidence that confirms the faith of our major religions in an afterlife. For this we are indebted to the painstaking research during the past century of a small group of brilliant scientists such as Dr. William James and Sir Oliver Lodge who became tireless explorers into the possibility of life beyond death. We are also beholden to a handful of gifted psychics such as Eileen Garrett and Mrs. Gladys Osborne Leonard whose incredible clairvoyance gave us graphic views of the next dimension. Also there is a small corps of dedicated medical doctors, psychiatrists and psychologists such as Dr. Raymond Moody Jr., Dr. Kenneth Ring and Dr. Michael Sabom whose objective studies during the past fifteen years into the near-death experiences of a multitude of people revealed that many were seemingly granted similar visions of our live to come.

For the mass of evidence concerning humankind's immortality we are indebted to several metaphysical research organizations in the United States and Great Britain. Their meticulous documentation of hundreds of authentic cases offers further proof of the continuity of life beyond death.

The evidence goes further than simply substantiating life after death. Testimony received from the Other Side indicates that there are dimensions beyond our mortal realm similar to the visionary forecasts of the major world religions. These testimonies speak of heavenly bliss, but also remorse, purgatory and even hell of a soul's own making. We have proof that for most of us, our lives and love will continue in another dimension beyond our earthly demise.

I, was once as agnostic and as skeptical as you may be on the subject of life after death. I, once tended to judge most psychics as either "phonies" or slightly to totally deranged. I prejudged their claims of contact with life on the Other Side as either self-delusion or downright fraud.

I shall try to present the strongest possible evidence to overcome your doubts and misgivings. I also, am aware as you are, that the psychic field is plagued with charlatans who for monetary gain deceive the grief-stricken with false messages of hope. Nevertheless, I am presenting some brief case studies of the work of a few rare, gifted psychics of whose integrity I have no doubt. The evidence they offer has been carefully researched and objectively seeks to substantiate the premise that our personal existence does not end with physical death.

Death, instead of being the end of life, the evidence tells us, *is simply the gateway to a new life, a graduation from earthly existence to a more beautiful life on a higher plane!*

My concern with death first came to me in full force at the age of 26 when I was an ambulance driver with the British 8th Army in the Egyptian and Libyan deserts during World War II.

In June and July of 1942, pushed by Field Marshall Rommel's Afrika Korp, the British desert forces were forced to retreat nearly 400 miles from Tobruk, Libya eastward across the Egyptian desert to El Alamein, a railroad crossing just 60 miles from Alexandria's suburbs. For three months the 8th Army valiantly held back Rommel's savage efforts to break through the El Alamein line seeking to capture the Suez Canal.

On October 23rd, under General Montgomery's new command, the British 8th launched its own massive counter-offensive along a thirty mile front with heavy artillery bombardment and round-the-clock aerial bombing clearing the way for tanks and infantry to move forward. Ten nights and days of murderous pounding overwhelmed the crack Afrika Korp and sent it into a frantic retreat. That was the beginning of the 8th Army's 1,400 mile drive westward across North Africa, putting down intermittent suicidal rear-guard holding actions by Rommel's troops all the way from El Alamein to Tripoli, Libya.

As one ambulance driver among many, I was a minuscule part of all this and became acquainted with death. On too many occasions during those months, I talked with my soldier comrades in the desert twilight enjoying their jokes and laughter and admiring their courage just before an attack - only to see the next morning some of their bodies being delivered in my ambulance for burial.

At El Alamein during the summer of 1942 I was temporarily attached to a New Zealand Casualty Clearing Station. One evening just before an attack I struck up a conversation with a young Kiwi stretcher-bearer. He spoke warmly, wistfully about his young wife and about his farm in New Zealand while I responded about life in "the good old U.S."

9

I felt I had made a good friend and I looked forward to seeing him the next day.

That night there were many casualties on both sides. Among the most severely wounded was my new friend, mercifully near death; he was totally unconscious with one arm gone and part of his chest torn away. He didn't last the night and the next day I helped bury him under six feet of Egyptian desert sand along with three other brave young men.

As we put his mangled body, stiff and heavy, inside a canvas sack, into his desert grave, a regimental padre said the usual hopeful Bible words over him, promising, "Even though a man dies, let us remember that he still lives. For as Jesus said, 'I am the Resurrection and the Life. He that believeth in Me, though he were dead, yet shall he live: and whosoever liveth and believeth in me shall never die.'"

As I listened to those words, familiar from too many similar services, I wondered to myself:

Where did his spirit go?

What happened to that fine, young soldier so full of life and love and joy - *where did his spirit really go?*

Another unforgettable incident, also at El Alamein, further deepened my wonder about death. In a terribly damaging noon-day raid, 50 German Stukas, despite our big Red Cross laid out on the sand, dive-bombed the trucks and tents surrounding the much larger medical and surgical tents and strafed the men in the chow line before the mess truck. Absolute chaos ensued over the entire area of the medical station.

After the dust cleared, I saw a cluster of men frantically waving their arms and shouting, "Ambulance!" Immediately, I drove my vehicle toward them. There I found four men horribly maimed by bomb shrapnel, including a captain with his middle torn open, so unspeakably wounded he should have been unconscious. When I rushed forward to help him, he motioned me away. Despite his ghastly wounds, he sharply ordered me,

10

"Don't waste time on me. This is it for me. Take care of the others. Take care of the others who still have a chance!"

I ignored his order and as fast as possible hauled him and the others back to the main surgical tent for immediate medical attention. Beyond all help, he died that night.

The rest of the day of the air raid and all that night, while life slowly ebbed from his mangled body, I found myself haunted by that gallant captain's words. I had become fairly used to death, but this was something different.

How strange it was, I thought to myself, that such power and beauty should show itself so brightly in the midst of the obscenities of war. Yet there it was - a fact of life - as real and explicit as the purest, objective scientific data. This was not just one rare instance - in many instances, when faced with death, men somehow became bigger than they had been. Whatever you choose to call it - selflessness, God's light within, the Higher Power - no matter what you name it, it clearly is one of our deepest impulses. Hopefully, it is there in every one of us - something Sacred, Holy, part of God.

The next day when I helped bury the captain along with a number of others, I asked myself:

Where did that spirit go?

Where did that selfless, flaming white courage go - where did that noble grace and beautiful spirit go?

This question has haunted me ever since my days as an ambulance driver with the British 8th Army. I believed then, and still believe, that the spirit of those men I buried in the desert simply left their bodies and went on to some other dimension beyond our present sight and knowledge. Certainly the spirit of that fine, young New Zealand stretcher-bearer was not in that sack of mangled flesh and bones we buried in the

11

desert sands. The courageous spirit of that incredible captain was not in the maimed and broken body inside the canvas sack we buried nearby.

I believe his spirit and the New Zealand stretcher-bearer's spirit - and the spirits of all the others - did not die, but continue their existence in a higher dimension.

Those whose only belief is in a material, finite world will find the belief in continuation of the personality beyond death unacceptable. They will argue that when a person dies, his brain dies along with the rest of his body. This, of course, is a fact. Consequently, they will insist that since the brain is the center of one's intelligence, when the brain is destroyed, there is no mentality. All that remains is a mindless, dead body.

Dr. Lawrence LeShan pointed out in his brilliant book, *The Medium, the Mystic and the Physicist* (1966): "It is very difficult for the modern scientist to think of the possibility of the personality surviving biological death because of his assumption that brain and mind are the same. This is accepted as the 'truth' and *it is rarely realized that this is an assumption and that other conceptualizations are possible.* For example, there is a viewpoint taken by Bergson, James, Eccles, Burt, and others which is perhaps best summed up in the words of Sir Charles Sherrington, 'Mental phenomena on examination do not seem amenable to understanding under physics and chemistry. I have therefore to think of the brain as an organ of liaison between energy and mind, but not as a converter of energy into mind and vice versa.'"[1] Sir Charles Sherrington received the 1932 Nobel Prize for medicine for his study of reflexes and his analysis of the integrative action of the nervous system, and is considered to be the father of neurophysiology.

12

Enlarging on LeShan's thesis, Sherwood Eddy in *You Will Survive After Death* (1950), notes that "William James and Henri Bergson endeavored to show that the mind overflows the brain, that the function of the brain is not productive of thought but merely transmissive, as in the case of the vocal chords in transmitting sound. They held that the human brain is but the temporary and imperfect instrument of the mind that survives it at death."[2]

The late Dr. Wilder Penfield, one of the world's foremost neurosurgeons, in his fascinating book, *The Mystery of the Mind*, (1975) concurred with LeShan, Sherrington and James, pointing out that "the mind seems to act independently of the brain in the same sense that a programmer acts independently of his computer."[3] His many years of extraordinary brain surgery, dealing with and often curing epileptics, led him to the conclusion that the mind was distinct from the brain and body, that it was a distinctive reality, that it had an energy of its own and was something not to be reduced to brain mechanism.

"...there is no good evidence," he declared, "...that the brain alone can carry out the work that the mind does, ...the mind must be viewed as a basic element in itself. One might call it a medium, an essence, a soma. That is to say, it has a continuing existence...[4] As Hippocrates expressed it long ago, 'the brain is messenger' to consciousness. Or as one might now express it, the brain's highest mechanism is 'messenger' between the mind and the other mechanisms of the brain...[5] A man's mind, one might say, is the person, he walks about the world, depending always upon his private computer which he programs continuously to suit his ever-changing purpose and interest."[6]

William James, often called the founder of modern psychology, author of the landmark books *Principles of Psychology*(1890) and *The Varieties of Religious Experience*(1902), a physician, psychologist and an eminent philosopher, was one of Harvard's star professors. As a leader

13

of both the British and the American Societies for Psychical Research, he pursued the question of survival after death for nearly forty years. He conducted scores of scientifically supervised seances with some of the most famous mediums of the 1890-1920 period. In *The Will to Believe and Human Immortality* he wrote:

"When the brain stops acting altogether, or decays, that special stream of consciousness which it subserved will vanish entirely from this material world. But the sphere of being that supplied the consciousness will still be intact and in the more real world with which even while here, it was continuous, the consciousness might, in ways unknown to us, continue still."[7]

Many metaphysicians have long thought we humans actually had two bodies - one, a physical, material body of flesh, blood and bone, the other, an astral or etheric body of spirit, of the feeling heart, mind and soul.

When the physical body dies, the individual continues in a more subtle form of matter, an astral body, which lives on - *is* mind - *is* feeling - *is* spirit. The human personality - which thinks - feels - loves - and cares - continues on another wave length - and perhaps at a higher frequency.

In other words, when our heart stops beating, our lungs stop breathing and our physical body no longer functions, it is my strong feeling, as well as that of many others, our astral body - our spirit - our emotional heart, mind and soul simply moves on to another dimension.

We do not "die." Nor do our loved ones when they "depart." Our loved ones - wife, husband, mother, father, daughter, son, intimate friends - do not leave us in "death." Though you may feel momentarily abandoned, they have not deserted you: their spirit - their feeling heart, mind and soul - are simply in a dimension we cannot see or hear.

Based on my research and personal psychic life experience, it is my firm conviction that this realm beyond death operates on a higher wave length than our normal sensitivities can perceive. It is my further conviction that this higher realm with its faster, more intense, vibrations has been penetrated, seen, heard and recorded by a small corps of gifted persons whom we call "sensitives" or "mediums."

Dr. Lawrence LeShan, again from his book, *The Medium, the Mystic and the Physicist,* says: "A sensitive is a person who demonstrates precognition, telepathy and/or clairvoyance with unusual frequency. A medium is a sensitive who explains her (most frequently in Western culture these are women) acquisition of paranormally gained information by saying she got it from 'spirits' or 'the souls of people who have already died.' Some mediums go into trance in which they identify themselves as being someone else. In trance a good medium will demonstrate a high level of paranormally acquired information."[8]

These gifted earthlings are the "receivers" of messages from the other side, just as radio and television receives wireless frequencies of a multitude of voices and images of people and places from hundreds and thousands of miles distance. Despite widespread skepticism and often scornful disbelief, communication between earthlings and discarnate spirits has been going on for thousands of years. It has been personally experienced, not surprisingly, by some of the world's most famous leaders and greatest geniuses.

Did you know that the great Greek philosopher, Socrates (470-399 B.C.) communicated with a spiritual guide he called Daemon whom he presumed to be from the Other Side?

"Socrates claimed that, at times, he was inspired by a control or 'daemon,'" Geraldine Cummins, a distinguished Irish medium and author, explains in her book, *Mind in Life and Death* (1955). "He used to place

15

himself in a special state of passivity necessary when he wished to listen to his daemon in order to obtain advice or inspiration. In our day it is described by the term 'control.' The 'control' or 'daemon' may be a secondary personality of the medium, or an expression of the subconscious self, or as Socrates seems to have believed, an inspiring spirit guardian: in other words, a distinct individual who existed apart from himself. Apparently it is the old idea of the guardian angel - in Greek mythology 'a supernatural being, lesser divinity or genius.'"[9]

The heresy of Socrate's belief in this invisible spirit Daemon and his steadfast refusal to repudiate its existence were among the factors which led to his conviction for "impiety" by the Greek state and finally to his martyr's death by drinking poisonous hemlock.

As a skeptic, you may easily dismiss Socrates' Daemon as an emotional disturbance, an hallucination, or the vision of a madman, as one 19th century psychiatrist, Dr. L. F. Le'lut, who dealt daily with the mentally ill in a Paris asylum, did in his book, *Du De'mon de Socrates* (1856).

But it is hard to as lightly dismiss the brilliance of Socrates' philosophical teachings which eventually transformed the thinking of the Western world. Nor can we dismiss the selfless sanity, humanity, beauty and simple goodness of his personal being - described by his students as "all glorious within." His most famous student, Plato, described him as "truly the wisest, and justest, and best of all men whom I have ever known...the most righteous man of the whole age." Nor is it possible to lightly dismiss the gallant courage and grace with which he faced his impending, inevitable execution.

As the time for his death drew near, only moments before the executioner brought to his cell the cup of hemlock which was to dispatch him, his many close friends who crowded the cell abandoned themselves completely to uncontrolled weeping. He alone remained calm.

As he awaited the hemlock, he quietly and subtly reminded them, albeit indirectly, of his firm belief in the immortality of the spirit, saying with a smile, "Be of good cheer - and say that you are burying my body only."

Only his body! For Socrates knew his spirit would live on.[10]

Did you know that President Lincoln and his wife Mary Todd were sustained in their overwhelming grief over the loss of their young son, Willie, through seances in the White House? At another White House seance, guidance from the Other Side moved President Lincoln to personally visit the Army of the Potomac when the fighting spirit of the troops was at its lowest ebb following the disaster at Fredericksburg. Adhering to the advice he received in the seance he also brought his wife and young son Tad with him to review the troops. There, in the midst of the utter despondency of the defeated soldiers, he talked individually with both with the enlisted men and the officers and visited the wounded, the ill and injured. His inspiring, caring, highly personal family visit, as predicted in the seance, turned the morale of that army completely around, so that some have described it as a turning point in the Civil War.

On yet another occasion, also in the White House, Lincoln was advised by a spirit voice resembling the deceased Senator Daniel Webster to hold firm and issue the Emancipation Proclamation despite strong opposition within his cabinet and Congress and widespread public outcry against it. In the seance, Lincoln was solemnly warned to neither soften the terms nor delay the enforcement. "It will be the crowning event of your administration and your life," the spirit voice told him.

On January 1, 1863, President Lincoln issued into law by presidential edict the Emancipation Proclamation freeing all the slaves in the Confederate states, a monumental step toward the ultimate elimination of all slavery within the United States. Thousands of American as well as many Europeans hailed Lincoln's move as a great act of statesmanship and it was, indeed, as the seance predicted,"the crowning event" of his presidency.[11]

"And 'way out' though it may seem," David C. Knight points out in *The ESP Reader* (1969) "There are those who claim the Proclamation itself was inspired from 'beyond.'"[12]

Nettie Colburn Maynard who was the medium in the seances cited above, in her book *Was Abraham Lincoln a Spiritualist?* (1891) noted that if Lincoln "had not had faith in spiritualism, he would never have connected himself with it...especially in peculiarly dangerous times while the fate of the Nation was in peril." But she frankly admitted that "had he declared an open belief in the subject, he would have been pronounced insane and probably incarcerated."[13]

Nevertheless, he took the risk of exploring the unknown and quietly searching for guidance not only from his personal God through daily prayers but also from human spirits on the Other Side. In this and in many other ways he was a spiritual kinsman to Socrates.

When the gifted, young, psychic medium Nettie Colburn Maynard first met Lincoln in 1962, she was struck, as she was many times afterward, by the deep sorrow that was written indelibly upon his face.

"I think I have never seen so sad a face in my life," she recalled, "and I have looked into many a mourner's face. I have been among bereaved families, orphan children, widows and strong men whose hearts have been broken by the taking away of their own; but I never saw the depth of sorrow that seemed to rest upon that gaunt but expressive countenance...he bore the world upon his heart."[14]

By 1864 the sadness was even more acute. As Socrates had done, he began to sense that his days on earth were already numbered.

All during the long agony of the war he had seemed to sense this. Recalling her visit with the president at the White House, the author of *Uncle Tom's Cabin* Harriet Beecher Stowe said she felt about him "a dry, weary, patient pain that many mistook for insensibility" as they talked about the war. When she spoke hopefully about the end of the war, he said matter-of-factly, without self pity and without feeling, "whichever way it ends, I have the impression I shan't last long after it's over."[15]

In the early April of 1865, Lincoln had a strange and troubling dream that unfortunately proved to be a prophetic vision. In that dream, which he related to his wife Mary, his close friend and bodyguard Federal Marshall Ward Hill Lamon and several other witnesses, as Lamon recorded it in his *Recollections of Abraham Lincoln* (1895), while he was sleeping the president first noted a deathlike stillness about the White House, then heard subdued sobs as if a number of people were weeping. In his dream, he wandered downstairs and again heard the same pitiful sobbing but the mourners were invisible.

Finally he entered the East Room where he was met with a sickening surprise. There before him was a catafalque on which nested a corpse in funeral vestments with soldiers stationed as guards about the body. A throng of people were gazing upon the corpse whose face was covered, others were weeping pitifully.

"Who is dead in the White House?" he demanded of one of the soldiers.

"The President," was his answer, "he was killed by an assassin."

Then a loud burst of grief from the crowd awakened him from his dream. Profoundly shocked by what he had witnessed clairvoyantly, he slept no more that night.[16]

Only a few days later, on April 15th, 1865, his prophetic dream was fulfilled - as we all know too well - when Lincoln was shot by John Wilkes Booth while attending a performance at the Ford Theatre and died the next morning. Secretary of War Edwin Stanton said - also prophetically - as he stood beside the president's bedside only moments after his passing: "Now he belongs to the ages."

Did you know that Thomas Alva Edison, America's most prolific and spectacular inventor, who discovered the electric light, who conceived the phonograph, who developed the alkaline battery, who improved the motion picture in myriad ways, who held patents for more than 1,000 creative inventions, was searching for an apparatus to contact the dead at the time of his death? He designed and made drawings of a machine to pick up, enlarge and amplify, the delicate communications which sensitive mediums receive from the Other Side.

Although he seldom spoke about faith or religion, Edison, the son of spiritualist parents, clearly believed in life after death. In his published *Diary and Sundry Observations* he revealed his motivation for the development of a machine that would help us contact the so-called "dead."

"I am inclined to believe that our personality in the hereafter will be able to affect matter," he wrote. "If this reasoning is correct, then, if we can evolve an instrument so delicate as to be affected or moved, or manipulated by our personality as it survives in the next life, such an instrument, when made available, ought to record something.."[17]

You could argue that we already have such an instrument in the old-fashioned ouija board, but obviously, Edison was thinking of an instrument more finely tuned, much more accurate.

A further insight into Edison's thinking regarding psychic research is given us by Dr. Miller Hutchinson, one of Edison's long time, intimate associates. In a conversation with Dr. S. Ralph Harlow, reported in his book *Life After Death* (1961), Dr. Hutchinson said: "Edison and I are convinced that in this field of psychical research will yet be discovered facts and data that will prove of greater significance to the thinking of the human race than all the inventions we have ever made in the field of electricity."[18]

When Edison died early one Sunday morning on October 18th, 1931 at 3:24 A.M., mysteriously, unaccountably, the office clocks of three of Edison's top associates at the Edison Laboratory each stopped at the exact time of his death - at 3:24 A.M.! Furthermore, the large wall clock in Edison's own office stopped at 3:27 A.M. - just three minutes later![19]

These three associates of their beloved friend Tom had no explanation as to why the clocks had stopped at exactly the same time in each of their offices. The night watchman of the Edison "Lab," was as amazed as everyone else by the phenomena and swore to Edison's son he hadn't gone near the clocks.

Adding a further complication to the puzzle was the fact that Edison had once recorded on both cylinders and disks (recording devices he had invented some years prior) one of his favorite songs, "Grandfather's Clock," which ended with the words "...But it stopped short, never to go again, when the old man died!"

Why did the three clocks stop at the exact time of Tom's death and the clock in his personal office stop three minutes later?[20] It is a mystery which, to date, no one has solved.

However, if you believe in life after death, perhaps the answer is that wily old Tom Edison, 82 years old at the time of his death, but still strong of mind and still possessed of his whimsical sense of humor, was trying to tell his associates he was still around - indeed, perhaps trying to tell us what he fervently believed - that our personality and spirit survive after death. Here, at last, shortly after he had crossed the threshold to the

21

Other Side, was a concrete and specific way whereby he could demonstrate to those who loved him that he still lived.

Did you know that Johannes Brahms (1833-1897), the renowned composer of some of the world's most sublime symphonies, frankly denied he personally created his own music but instead, received those gorgeous chords and exquisite melodies of his greatest compositions from a Higher Source while he was in a state of semi-trance?

Before confessing this to a young writer who was seeking to discover the relationship of inspiration to genius for an article, Brahms exacted a solemn promise from the aspiring author that whatever he said would not be publicized until at least fifty years after his death.

A three-hour interview was held in Brahms' Vienna home in the late fall of 1896, less than six months before the composer's death. It was taken down verbatim by an expert stenographer from the American Embassy in Vienna, and witnessed by the illustrious violinist, Joseph Joachim who was Brahms' dear friend. It contains revelations, so startling that one can understand Brahms' reluctance to have these disclosures made known to the skeptical, rationalistic world in which he lived.

The young writer, an American named Arthur M. Abell, finally published the interview as part of a small book entitled *Talks With Great Composers,* put out by G. E. Schroeder-Verlag in West Germany in 1964, sixty seven years after the interview. Although to me an inspiring book, it was never a best seller and is now out of print.

Explaining in more detail exactly what went on within his psyche during the creative act of composing, Brahms said, "...when I felt those higher cosmic vibrations I knew I was in touch with the same Power that inspired those great poets, Goethe, Milton and Tennyson as well as the musicians, Bach, Mozart and Beethoven. Then the ideas which I was consciously seeking flowed in upon me with such force and such speed that I could only grasp and hold a few of them; I never was able to jot them down; they came in instantaneous flashes and quickly faded away again unless I fixed them on paper. *The themes that will endure in my compositions all come to me in this way.* It has always been such a wonderful experience that I never before could induce myself to talk about it - even to you, Joseph," he confided to his good friend Joachim. "I felt that I was, for the moment, in tune with the Infinite, and there is no thrill like it!"[21]

Brahms is not the only creative genius to acknowledge the source of his inspiration as a force far greater than himself.

George Frederick Handel (1685-1759) wrote 41 Italian-style operas which were popular in their day but are rarely played today. At 53 years of age, after suffering a stroke, he turned to composing "The Messiah" and in doing so found himself inspired in a way that he had never before experienced. Some critics have called this work the greatest single piece of music composed by man. When "The Messiah" was premiered in London, the audience, including the king and his entourage, was so uplifted by the "Hallelujah Chorus" that it rose spontaneously to its feet at the climax.

Badly depressed before he undertook "The Messiah," Handel created it in but 24 feverish days. Never leaving his room, often forgetting to eat, at times moved to tears by what he wrote, throughout the brief span of 24 days he felt electrified by the fever of creativity. Exhausted and exalted on the completion of the work, and awed by the fact that he knew it was a masterpiece surpassing anything he had previously written, he said to his friends:

"I have seen Heaven and God Himself!"[22]

Did you know that Moses Maimonides (1135-1204) - called by the *Encyclopedia Judaica* "the most illustrious figure in Judaism in the post-Talmudic era and one of the greatest of all times...and regarded as *the supreme rationalist*"[23] - nevertheless declared his fervent belief in the spiritual bliss of the soul in the afterlife?

As the record of his genius as a philosopher, physician, lawyer, rabbi and spiritual leader of his people eloquently witnesses, Moses Maimonides was truly, to use Shakespeare's phrase, "a man for all seasons." Since his death nearly 800 years ago, the legendary aura of his greatness has kept alive within Jewish homes throughout the world the popular saying: "From Moses to Moses, there is no one like Moses!"

Judaism's commitment to a faith in survival after death is as profound and unswerving as is that of Christianity. The comment on "Afterlife" in the *Encyclopedia Judaica* begins with this unequivocal statement: "Judaism has always maintained a belief in an afterlife." Orthodox Jews daily recite during grace and after meals the prayer: "May the All-merciful make us worthy of the days of Messiah, and of the life of the world to come." The Reform-Jewish movement in a special passage in its Pittsburgh Platform is equally firm in its belief in the hereafter: "we reassert the doctrine of Judaism that the soul is immortal, grounding this belief in the divine nature of the human spirit..."[24]

Although written over 800 years ago, Maimonides' treatment of spiritual bliss in the hereafter in his Code (Yad, Teshuvah 8) is much more explicit:

> *There is no way at all for us in this world to know or comprehend the great goodness which the soul experiences in the world to come, for in this world we know only of material pleasures and it is these we desire....in reality there can be no way of comparing the good of the soul in the world to come with the physical goods of food and drink in this world.*

As though he had a vision of the afterlife similar to the near-death experiences documented in this century by the studies of Drs. Raymond Moody, Kenneth Ring, Michael Sabom and others, Maimonides went on to say of "the great goodness which the soul experiences in the world to come,"

> *That good is great beyond all our understanding and incomparable beyond all our imagination.*[25]

Like those who experienced near-death visions in our time, he, too, found his view of the afterlife so magnificent it was "ineffable!"

Would you be surprised to know that over two centuries ago, one of the world's greatest philosophers, noted for the clarity and logic of his reasoning, predicted the close range acquaintance of our "immortal souls" with "far distant globes of the cosmic system?"

Immanuel Kant (1724-1804) is considered one of the most important thinkers of modern times. A distinguished professor of logic and metaphysics at the University of Königsberg, he was most famous for his philosophical study, *Critique of Pure Reason.* In that study Kant has some startling things to say about humankind's immortality, noting that our present world is much more complex and limitless than we humans perceive it to be:

> *If we could see ourselves and other objects as they* ***really are****, we should see ourselves in a world of spiritual natures, our community which neither began at our birth nor will end with the death of the body.*

Continuing, Kant said that although we are unaware, communications with the spiritual world are already going on:

> *At some future day it will be proved - I cannot say when and where - that the human soul is, while in the earth life, already in uninterrupted communication with those living in another world; that the human soul can act upon those beings, and receive in return, impressions of them without being conscious of it in the ordinary personality.*[26]

Did you know that the man whose incisive, brilliant command of the RAF in 1940 saved Britain from invasion by the Nazis was also deeply involved in psychic exploration and later became the author of four notable books on the subject of life after death?

The victory of Air Chief Marshall Hugh Dowding and the Royal Air Force over Göring's overpowering Luftwaffe bomber fleets has been compared to Lord Nelson's defeat of Napoleon's sea forces at the Battle of Trafalgar. From August 13th, 1940 when Hitler decided to invade England by throwing the entire force of the Luftwaffe against the RAF, until October 11th when he finally called off his projected invasion, - for nearly two months of frightening days and sleepless, horrible nights - 500 to 1,000 Nazi bombers *daily* marrauded Britain's coastline, airfields and cities. Under Dowding's command RAF airmen in Spitfire and Hurricane fighter planes, aided by a radar early warning system, intercepted and shot down over 1,700 Nazi bombers - more than half the German airforce! That cost was so great that even madman Hitler angrily realized he had lost the Battle of Britain.

Winston Churchill, acknowledging Air Chief Marshall Dowding as the architect of that victory, said of him: "We must regard the generalship here shown as an example of genius in the art of war."

Alluding to the courage of those extra-ordinary RAF airmen, who were inspired by the valor of their commander, he paid this now famous tribute: "Never in the field of human conflict has so much been owed by so many to so few!" It was not an over-statement. Thanks to their efforts, Hitler had been stopped, his proposed invasion postponed - as it turned out - forever, and *Great Britain had been saved*!

Britain's tragic loss was that out of "the Few" as they came to be called, one out of three of those RAF airmen - nearly 1,000 - were wounded or killed!

The loss of those gallant young men hit Dowding very hard. He was noted for his care and concern for the men under his command. The loyalty and devotion they returned to him was a major factor in the RAF victory over the Luftwaffe. Yet 449 of his fighter pilots, whom he regarded as part of his family, had flown to their death repelling the Nazis. Out of that deep involvement with those airmen it became Dowding's destiny to give most of the rest of his life to the study of the evidence of survival after death.

During that time, from his retirement at age 60 until his death at 87 he wrote four stunning books, *Many Mansions* (1943), *Lychgate* (1945), *God's Magic* (1948) and *The Dark Star* (1951). Although it was contrary

27

to his modest nature, he became a star platform performer before psychic and spiritualist gatherings. He also worked closely with a small circle of gifted psychic people - both earthlings and souls from the Other Side - to increase our understanding of the continuity of life.

As he wrote in *God's Magic*:

> *Communication with those who have passed the boundary of death, and have actually experienced the conditions of which they speak, is quite obviously a means of information which we shall be very foolish to ignore, provided we can satisfy ourselves that such communication is possible...All that I, or anyone else, can fairly claim is that discarnate communication is one of the most valuable and prolific methods by which humanity may attain to some approximation to knowledge on the other side of physical death, and that those who refuse to avail themselves of this potential source of information are deliberately ignoring something of great importance to themselves...*

> *Conviction comes normally by an almost unnoticed accretion of evidence which piles up if the subject is continuously studied... We lose all fear of death as soon as we become convinced of the fact of immediate conscious and active survival. Proof of survival is the beginning and not the end of the road.*

> *If you can get what I have got out of discarnate communication, it will be something that alters your whole view of life and death, and life*

after death. The mere realization that life and consciousness are continuous on both sides of death is of tremendous important. ...The evidence which has convinced me...is available to anyone who cares to investigate with an open mind.[27]

The Holy Bible is a veritable source book of supernormal psychic experiences including clairvoyance through dreams and visions, visitations by angels, and even direct communication with God. From the myriad, fantastic instances in the Old Testament, let us look at the case of Moses. As the greatest of the Biblical prophets, a passionate liberator, wise law-giver and a great statesman, Moses is the classic example of a man inspired by a Higher Power to play a role in history far beyond his mortal, human capacity!

The great epic in the Biblical accounts of Moses leading the children of Israel from slavery to freedom in the Promised Land is a recital of miracle after miracle and a running dialogue between God and man. Yahweh (the Hebrew word for God) spoke to Moses out of a burning bush telling him of his destiny to free the Jewish people from their enslavement to the Egyptian Pharaoh, Rameses II. Subsequently, Yahweh had to bring ten plagues on the stubborn Pharaoh before he would agree to release the Israelites. Then Yahweh guided Moses and his fleeing slaves across the desert to the Red Sea, spreading its water so that the children of Israel might walk on the floor of the sea while the Egyptian troops who pursued them were drowned. Three months later, from the heights of Mount Sinai, Yahweh gave Moses the Ten Commandments - the foundation of Israel's nationhood and religion.

For Moses to bring a vast number of his people from serfdom to freedom was a miraculous act of leadership and a testament to his genius and almost inexhaustible patience. However, he reached the zenith in his spiritual development when he acted as a medium in receiving the Ten Commandments. To this God-inspired, incredible human being, we owe the Jewish-Christian monotheistic concept of one transcendent God, the conviction that killing and theft are crimes against society, the rejection of the worship of idols and graven images as a monstrous abhorrence, the Sabbath as a weekly day of rest for the health and welfare of the working masses, the ideals of caring love and honor for one's family and respect of one's neighbor. These are crucial concepts for a harmonious community, the basic code of moral laws embodied in the Ten Commandments. Even today, they constitute the basic, though still unrealized, ethics of most Western civilized states.

Like the account of Moses, the story of Jesus in the four gospels of the Bible's New Testament, is another mosaic of one psychic, supernormal phenomenon after another, forming a picture of an incredibly beautiful, loving human being who was a compassionate brother to all humankind.

Of Jewish parentage and Jewish heritage, he assured the patriarchs of his culture, "Do not think I have come to destroy the Law or the Prophets. I have not come to destroy, but to fulfill."[28] Time after time, he repeated in his teachings the commandments of the Old Testament, "Thou shalt love the Lord thy God" from Deuteronomy and "Thou shalt love they neighbor as thyself" from Leviticus.

Jesus demonstrated the great commandment of love by his life - love lived in him; indeed, God His Father lived in him. As he conducted his countless healings and other miracles - giving the blind their sight, restoring the tortured insane to the peace of sanity, cleansing the leper, healing the crippled who joyously threw away their crutches and walked, feeding a multitude with a few loaves and fishes, bringing Lazarus back to life from the grave - he humbly explained to his disciples that he was merely a medium for God's power: "the Father dwelling in me, it is He who does the works."[29]

Later, he assured his disciples in equally humble words, "Truly, truly, I say to you, he who believes in me will also do the works that I do; and greater works than these will he do..."[30] All his great works were simply a demonstration of what can happen when the inner spirit of each us us is truly opened to the full power of God's infinite love.

Three days after his crucifixion by the Romans and his burial in a tomb, he personified the truth of immortality by his resurrection, the primary postulate upon which the Christian Church was founded.

The greatest miracle of Jesus is not the world-wide church which was founded in his name - the greatest miracle is the fact that such an incredibly wondrous human being actually existed! To those who doubt his existence and call his story pure mythology, Will Durant, philosopher, historian and author of the eleven-volume world history *The Story of Civilization,* offers this intriguing response:

> "That a few simple men should in one generation have invented so powerful and appealing a personality, so lofty an ethic and so inspiring a vision of human brotherhood would be a miracle far more incredible than any recorded in the Gospel!"[31]

31

In the pages that follow I will present a few case studies, carefully chosen for their meticulous documentation, which will further unfold the beautiful mystery of life and love beyond death. I fervently hope that these cases by persons of highest integrity and unimpeachable veracity - plus my own experiences - will not only help you in your "unbelief" but will ultimately prove to you beyond all doubt that God's greatest gift to his children on earth is *the eternal life that lies ahead for you and for me and for all of our loved ones.*

*Raymond Lodge, soldier, son
of eminent scientist Sir Oliver
Lodge, after death in Flanders,
assures his family of his happy
life on the Other Side.*

There were nearly nine million young men killed in World War I. The finest sons of Great Britain and its far-flung empire, France, Germany, Austria, Hungary, Belgium, Holland, Italy, Russia and the United States - the best and the bravest - were slaughtered in that ghastly war. Among them was Raymond Lodge, the son of one of England's most distinguished physicists - Sir Oliver Lodge.

Killed in action in France, Raymond moved on to the next dimension, then through gifted psychic mediums sought out by his father, returned to earth to tell his loved ones about life "over there."

Prior to his untimely death, Sir Oliver's son Raymond was a brilliant, handsome, joyous young man with a strong bent for engineering and mechanics. After studying engineering at the University of Birmingham, he took a two year senior apprenticeship at the Wolseley Motor Car Company. Next he joined a firm specializing in automobile spark plugs called Lodge Plugs, Ltd., which had been founded by his two older brothers.

When World War I broke out, the invading armies of Kaiser Wilhelm's military machine swept like a scourge through Belgium and Holland and then on into France. Raymond volunteered for the British Army in September, 1914 and was commissioned as a Second Lieutenant in a crack infantry regiment, the South Lancashires.

Following six months of rigorous training, he was sent to the

33

battlefront in France. For the next six months, except for brief periods of leave, he lived in the frontline dugouts and trenches. He learned to accept those inevitable parts of his soldier's life, the rats, mud and spartan conditions of underground existence. To these conditions there was added the nerve-rattling strain of sporadic shellfire, and the intermittent bursts of machine guns with the resulting casualties. With the passage of time there was the ever-growing stench of the irretrievable, unburied dead in the no-man's-land between the two warring armies.

His letters home were cheerful, thoughtful, always concerned for his comrades beside him and his cherished family at home. Humorous, self-depreciating and uncomplaining in tone, his communications to his loved ones reflected a gallant, heroic young man who, even in the trenches, managed to find moments that were amusing, touching, or in other ways worthwhile. Hemingway defined courage as "grace under pressure." Raymond Lodge's conduct during those awful months was a demonstration of that grace.

As he was leading his men back from the frontline trenches one morning, a burst of shrapnel tore into his back, leaving him terribly wounded. A few hours later he died - around noon of September 14th, 1915 - and was buried by the side of a road. His death was just a year from the time he had volunteered.

At the time of Raymond's death, Sir Oliver Lodge was a world famous scientist and leader in many other fields, a man who seemed to have everything. He had a lovely, helpful wife, a wonderful family of six sons and six daughters, and was loved by all who knew him. In addition, he was respected and admired by many thousands who were acquainted with his good works, speeches and extensive writings.

Knighted for his outstanding work in atomic and electrical theory, he had been applauded in the scientific community for his investigations into lightning, its conductors and guards, electrolysis, the speed of the ion, and electro-magnetic waves.

He had pioneered in wireless telegraphy at about the same time as the acclaimed inventor, Guglielmo Marconi. Lodge had not only discovered the wireless principle and taken out a patent on his invention, but had also organized a company for its commercial development. As a consequence, the Marconi Company approached him, bought out his company in 1911 for £20,000 sterling and retained Lodge as a consultant for seven years at £1,000 sterling per year.[1]

It was typical of the spirit of Lodge that, having discovered the principle of wireless telegraphy, he was ready to relinquish his claims to ownership so that he could be free to delve into other undiscovered but fascinating mysteries. Among his other concerns were education, government, human rights, women's suffrage, religion and psychic research. For nearly 15 years he served as Principal of Birmingham University. He was an outspoken leader of the British Society for Psychical Research. In popular writing in magazines and newspapers he sought to reconcile the differences between science and religion.

Expressing his belief in the possibility of earthlings communicating with the dead, in 1909 he wrote a book, *The Survival of Man,* further emphasizing that conviction. This book was dedicated to the founders of the Society for Psychical Research whom he called "the truest and most patient workers in an unpopular region of science." This book presented numerous documented accounts of paranormal phenomena from telepathy to alleged conversations with persons from the Other Side. It also included his personal testimony of seances, which he and other investigators had witnessed, during which lucid moments of communication occurred between the living and so-called "dead."

35

All of this was far-out moondust to many of his scientific colleagues. In their opinion, the psychic field was the domain of mad spiritualists and other "kooks" of the lunatic fringe. Any attempt by a reputable scientist of lesser stature than Sir Oliver to scientifically investigate life after death would have been derided and publicly ridiculed.

Despite such opposition, Sir Oliver had the courage to venture "where angels fear to tread." Because of his great stature as a scientist, leaders of that community could not intimidate him; as a devout member of the Church of England, the church hierarchy did not dare to try to silence him. Both the scientific and religious communities could only respectfully - and sometimes not too respectfully - disagree with him while he tenaciously continued his investigations into this taboo realm.

The general reading public, however, welcomed his book. They respected his achievements as a scientist and his integrity as a Christian layman. They were warmed by his modest, friendly demeanor and impressed by the scientific methods of the Society for Psychical Research which he embraced. They admired him for having the courage to explore this forbidden, undefined territory, about which they too had wondered. They applauded him for searching for scientific proof of the widely professed but still nebulous belief in humankind's immortality.

These people bought his book, read it avidly, recommended it to friends and pushed its sales through several editions. Clearly, the public wanted to know more about life beyond this life. This was especially true at the time when World War I brought the sorrow of death to millions of homes.

When Raymond was killed, Sir Oliver was momentarily shattered, as we all are, by the loss of a loved one. At first, the demise of his beloved son seemed almost too much to bear. Nevertheless, knowing that Raymond was alive in a realm beyond this earth, he regained the courage to continue his this-world existence. Now, more than ever, he felt compelled to prove the truth of his conviction that life continues after our earthly sojourn.

If there *really was* life after death, then this was the time to prove it! Not just to demonstrate to his colleagues in science and the church how incomplete was their knowledge - but far more important, to help all the millions who must experience the same throat-aching sorrow in the loss of a beloved one that he and his family were now enduring.

Perhaps, he thought humbly, this quest might also help assuage the terrible grief that had plunged him and his family into a deep depression and filled their home with a pall of gloom.

As a scientist, Sir Oliver was keenly aware of the predominance of frauds who professed to be genuine mediums. Truly gifted mediums were as rare in Lodge's time as they are today. Such psychic geniuses as Leonore Piper and Eileen Garrett were, like geniuses in other fields, incredibly developed, extraordinarily sensitive and very few in number.

Referring to the many people who claim that *all* mediums are frauds, Dr. William James, Sir Oliver's friend and colleague in psychic research, once wisely noted: "If you wish to upset the law that all crows are black, you must not seek to show that no crows are, it is enough if you prove a single crow to be white."[2]

Thus, even if a majority of mediums are frauds, if only one truly gifted medium can demonstrate verifiable contacts with persons who have "died," that is sufficient to prove the case for life after death. Leonore Piper, closely tested by members of both the British and American Societies for Psychical Research and particularly by Dr. James, proved to be his "white crow" in investigations.

Similarly, in his quest for authentic word from his "deceased" son Raymond, Sir Oliver discovered his own "white crows," Mrs. Katherine

37

Kennedy, Mr. Alfred Vout Peters and Mrs. Gladys Osborne Leonard. All three were persons of scrupulous honesty and highest integrity.

Mrs. Katherine Kennedy was a medium with the gift of automatic writing. She had discovered this gift a little over a year before Raymond's death when her beloved son Paul was tragically killed in an accident. Much to her amazement and joy, Paul had managed to communicate with her through her own hand via automatic writing - or so she thought. Fearful she might be deceiving herself, she wrote to Sir Oliver seeking his guidance concerning this phenomenon.

Gallantly, Sir Oliver saw Mrs. Kennedy, read her son Paul's messages, was deeply impressed, and encouraged her to develop her new-found gift. He personally took her anonymously to an American medium practicing in London, a Mrs. Wriedt, who gave her unmistakable proof that Paul still lived. Months later, on her own, Mrs. Kennedy received further confirmation of Paul's survival from two other mediums whom she herself had discovered. By remarkable coincidence, they were Alfred Vout Peters and Mrs. Gladys Osborne Leonard! When Sir Oliver asked her in late September of 1915 to help him reach Raymond she readily assented.[3]

Alfred Vout Peters was a keenly perceptive, highly respected trance medium and a popular, thought-provoking lecturer before London spiritualist circles. He had been a serious researcher of parapsychology for more than two decades.[4]

Mrs. Gladys Osborne Leonard, although only 33 years of age, went on to become one of the most trusted of all trance mediums during the next 50 years. Not only did she help many people like Sir Oliver and his family, but she subsequently became one of the most thoroughly investigated and carefully documented trance mediums in the annals of both the British and American Societies for Psychical Research. Despite the great fame which came to surround her she remained throughout her long life the same comely, thoughtful lady of dignity and common sense that Sir Oliver discovered when he first sought her help in communicating with Raymond.[5]

In his choice of the three gifted persons Sir Oliver asked to help him reach Raymond, he could not have been more fortunate.

Raymond came through!

Utilizing the instrumentalities of these three gifted mediums, he not only spoke to his father and his mother and later to his brothers and sisters, but also gave clear and accurate evidence of his past life and of the conditions of his present existence.

With his background in the effects of electricity on chemicals, electro-magnetic waves and the wireless, Sir Oliver dealt with the development of precise data. He carried this same scrupulous manner into studying the authenticity of these communications with his deceased son. Every word spoken in many seances was carefully transcribed and then painstakingly analyzed. He only accepted as authentic those things which Raymond revealed which were previously unknown to the medium and others in the seance; these items were declared "evidential material."

It became obvious on a number of occasions that Raymond was trying to help his father verify his identity. Raymond frequently volunteered personal information of which neither the medium nor Sir Oliver nor others attending the seance had any knowledge. But only after Sir Oliver had researched this information and found it to be correct did he consider it to be evidential.

The acid test of a medium's gift is the accuracy of the information relayed from the alleged spirit being contacted during a seance. No matter how trivial or inconsequential this information may seem to be, the verification of its truth or falseness can quickly determine whether the spirit communicator is who he or she claims to be.

Just a few among many specific evidential details whose accuracy seemed to prove Raymond's identity were the following:

1. Raymond mentioned the name of a fellow officer, an aeroplane specialist - a Lt. E. H. Mitchell of the Royal Flying Corps. It was obvious to Sir Oliver that his son did this for identification purpose because neither Sir Oliver nor the three mediums he was primarily dealing with had ever heard the name. Turning to government sources, it turned out there *was* such a Lt. Mitchell in the British air force. When Sir Oliver wrote to him, the young flying officer warmly responded that he had enjoyed meeting Raymond several months before, was grieved to learn of his death and extended the family his heartfelt condolences. A trivial detail perhaps yet certainly Raymond's identification of Lt. E. H. Mitchell was clearly evidential.

2. On another occasion, probing for evidence of Raymond's identity, Sir Oliver asked Raymond's alleged spirit to spell out the name of any of his brothers. At first Raymond spelled out the name NORMAN which seemed to Sir Oliver to be a mistake, then went on to spell out NOEL which was the name of one of his brothers.

Afterwards, discussing the matter with sons Alec and Noel, Sir Oliver learned that Norman was actually a comprehensive name for any or all of his brothers. Raymond was a hockey enthusiast and often spurred on his brothers with "Go to it, Norman!" or "Give it to them, Norman!"

Sir Oliver had asked Raymond to give him the name of any of his brothers and clearly his response covered all of them. Who, except for Raymond, could have responded as he did?

3. Another small detail of evidence indicated that Raymond was the communicator. In a seance involving his brother Alec, when Raymond

teasingly reminded him that somebody's birthday was coming up on January 25th, Alec responded,"You don't have to tell me!" It was Raymond's own birthday. He would be 27.

4. In another seance involving Alec, Raymond recalled to his brother how they used to talk a lot about cars - indeed they never tired of talking about cars. It was a passion for both of them.

5. Raymond joked about how he fancied he could sing. This was true; he was quite a fine singer. He acknowledged, however, that the hymn singing at prayer meetings just wasn't his line, but on songs like "Irish Eyes" and "My Orange Girl" he could really put himself into it. This was true; only Raymond could have said it. When Raymond mentioned "My Orange Girl," Alec sadly remembered it was the last piece of music Raymond had bought prior to his going to the trenches.

Perhaps the most convincing piece of evidence proving that the Raymond speaking in the seances was actually Sir Oliver's son concerned a missing photograph of him with some fellow officers taken a few weeks before his death.

Neither Sir Oliver nor Lady Mary nor any of his brothers or sisters nor any of the mediums involved in Raymond's case knew anything about this photograph until Raymond mentioned it during an anonymous seance with medium Vout Peters and Lady Mary September 27, 1915. He told Peters it was a group photo of himself with some of his fellow officers, and he said he had his walking stick with him. Peters emphasized to Lady Mary that "He particularly asked me to tell you this."

No one in the family knew of any such photograph and Mrs. Lodge expressed her skepticism about it later, thinking it was just a guess on Peters' part. Nevertheless, Sir Oliver conscientiously did his best to check out this bit of information, but was unsuccessful in tracking down any word about it.

41

On November 29th, Lady Lodge received a letter from a total stranger to the Lodge family - a Mrs. P.B.Cheves - whose son had been a medical officer to Raymond's regiment. She said her son had sent her half a dozen copies of a photograph of a group of officers and wondered if Lady Lodge knew of this photo. If not, she would be glad to send her one. She told Lady Lodge how often she had thought of her since her great sorrow and expressed her heartfelt sympathy.

Lady Lodge replied at once, thanking Mrs. Cheves for her thoughtfulness and asked for a copy of the photo.

On December 3rd, Sir Oliver, having now received a clue regarding the missing photo, decided to pursue the matter further in a seance with Mrs. Leonard. In this seance, Raymond described the photo more fully. He said there were a number of men in the picture - a mixed lot - officers of several companies. The photo was taken with a shed or shelter as a backdrop. The participants were in three rows, the first row squatted on the ground, the second seated on a long bench and the third standing behind them. He was in the front row, his walking stick at his feet, and the man behind him was leaning on his shoulder.

Sir Oliver deliberately did not mention to his son that the photo he was describing might already be in the mail from Mrs. Cheves; he wanted to test whether Raymond's delineation would match the actual photo.

On December 6th, Lady Mary, looking over Raymond's pack of personal things that had been sent to his home from the trenches, came upon his blood-stained diary with the notation on August 2th, "Photo taken."

On December 7th, a 9 x 12 photo arrived from Mrs. Cheves. It was a photo of officers in uniform. A shed served as the background. There were three rows of officers with Raymond in the front row squatted on the ground, his walking stick at his feet, a fellow officer immediately behind him leaning on Raymond's shoulder. It was exactly as Raymond had described on September 27th and more fully on December 3rd!

Evaluating this incident of the missing photograph some months later, Sir Oliver happily noted that it was exactly the sort of proof of Raymond's existence that he vigilantly sought. In his carefully understated style, he called the whole incident - particularly the "supernormally acquired" testimony he had received from Raymond - "rather exceptionally good as a piece of evidence."

There were other instances of evidential proof that were equally impressive. From beyond the grave, Raymond patiently and happily provided his beloved father with evidential material for psychical research purposes.

Of equal moment to those who are interested in the human and spiritual aspects of Raymond's life after death, his communications in the seances give us a picture of a charming, joyful and loving young man with a ready wit, an appetite for good-humored pranks and a deep and continued devotion to his mother and father and his brothers and sisters.

Although officially dead and buried, with a church memorial tablet reading, "...killed in action in Flanders about noon on Wednesday September 14th in the year of our Lord 1915," his communications revealed him to be a highly sensitive, deeply spiritual human being who was fascinated by life in the new realm beyond earthly existence.

Here is the essence of his comments concerning life on the Other Side transcribed from the seance-dialogues with his father, mother and other members of the family:

He spoke of his work with "dead" soldiers and said the war was not yet over for him:

Sir Oliver's first meeting with Raymond was in a seance with Mrs. Leonard only thirteen days after his death. Raymond made it clear to his father that he still felt a duty to help his fellow soldiers who had been killed in battle. Finding them wakened after death, they often were still haunted with fear and some even tried to go on fighting. He felt it was his task to explain to these soldiers what had happened to them and to assure them that they still lived although on another plane.

Buoyed by this assurance, when speaking at a public memorial service three days later, Sir Oliver was able to close his eulogy with an expression of firm faith, "Raymond has entered another region of service now...and we know his activity is not over."

At that time only Sir Oliver and his immediate family knew that this information had come to him from Raymond himself.

In another seance with his brother Lionel and Mrs. Leonard (Nov.17,1915) Raymond repeated what he deemed to be his immediate mission - to help and encourage "the poor chaps who have been literally shot into the spirit world" and could not understand what had happened to them.

He applauded his father's psychical research into survival after death, promised to give him irrefutable evidence and urged him to speak out boldly about that evidence. He said it would reassure millions on earth and help millions more who felt forgotten on the Other Side.

Lady Mary also had a seance with Alfred Vout Peters in which Raymond lauded his father's research and promised to help him document evidence which would be beyond contradiction. Heretofore, Raymond noted, his father's psychical research, his writing and speeches on the subject, had been largely intellectual. Now, he said elatedly, what his father wrote on the subject would be a matter of the heart and its personal eloquence would touch the hearts of millions.

44

In another seance about a month later with Sir Oliver and Mr. Peters (Oct.29,1915) he urged his father to put his full strength and all the persuasiveness of his personality into bringing his research to public attention. He assured his father the irrefutable evidence would override the quibbles of skeptics and help the Society for Psychical Research take a positive stand. He told his father that if he could see the many men and women who felt sadly forgotten on the Other Side because their relatives and friends on earth had no real belief in immortality, he would realize the importance of what he was doing. He joyously prophesied that thanks to his father's careful research, many millions both on earth and the Other Side would benefit from his passing and his after-death experiences.

He frequently expressed his deep and continuing love for his family and begged them to not grieve for him - for their unhappiness made him unhappy. He told them to rejoice - as he did - in the fact the he could still be with them.

Sir Oliver and Lady Mary were a devoted couple for more than fifty years and their love was reflected in their closely knit family of twelve wonderful children, first six boys and then six girls. As a family they enjoyed many festive occasions prior to Raymond's death.

Raymond was the youngest of the boys at the time of his death at 26; his older brothers were all engaged in engineering, commerce and the professions and his sisters were already in their teens or older. They all adored their young brother and were devastated by his death.

Prior to his passing, Sir Oliver's children, including Raymond, had shown little interest in their father's explorations of the paranormal and life beyond death. They were involved in youthful enterprises of more physical satisfaction such as hockey, tennis, sailing, their new motor cars, traveling abroad, the latest popular songs, new dance steps and the myriad other recreational pastimes of their upper class social set.

After Raymond's death, they became engrossed in the subject of humankind's survival. The early seances with Raymond and the family discussions afterward helped reconcile the remaining Lodge children to the fact that he was no longer physically with them.

About a month before Christmas (Nov.26,1915) in a seance with Lady Mary and Mrs. Leonard, Raymond spoke about how happy he was and so much more so because his darling mother was also happy - particularly now that she seemed convinced that he still lived. *He could not be happy when she was unhappy,* he told her.

Raymond offered to make a bargain with her - he promised he would be with the whole family on Christmas Day *provided there was no sadness or weeping.* Jokingly, he said *he didn't want to be a ghost at a feast. He didn't want to see any long faces, or tears, or hear any sad sighs.* He entreated his mother to rally up the family spirits now that they knew he still lived!

When his mother bravely promised him that they would all drink to his health and happiness on Christmas Day, he pledged that he would be there by her side, returning the toast and wishing them all his warmest wishes and great joy.

About a week later (Dec.3rd,1915) in a seance with Sir Oliver and Mrs. Leonard, Raymond reassured his father of his happiness, then blessed all of his family and told his father how very much he loved him. He said he couldn't adequately say what he felt - he felt so full of love he couldn't find the words to express it - and he felt so fortunate that he could still be with his family!

In another seance with his father and Mrs. Kennedy two weeks later, Sir Oliver mentioned to his son that Christmas was drawing near. Raymond said he expected to be with the family all that day but warned his father he must do his utmost to keep it jolly or it would hurt him horribly. He said he knew how difficult it was but everyone in the family must know by now that he was splendid - not only alive, but happy and just splendid!

Unfortunately, Raymond commented sadly, there would be thousands and thousands of departed soldiers like himself back in their homes on that day who would not be welcomed because their loved ones simply wouldn't realize they were still alive. He was so grateful his family was keeping a place for him that day! In closing, he once again blessed his father and sent his love to the family, said he must go now - and suddenly was gone.

The warm love for his family that Raymond reflected in these seances was also expressed on other occasions. Raymond showed his sensitive awareness of what his family members were doing - noting their anxieties, illnesses and sorrows as well as their joys and successes. *Clearly, even after death Raymond kept closely in touch with his family!*

He spoke of the conditions of his new life and was amazed and pleased at the physical similarities between his life in the next realm and life on earth.

In a seance with his brother Lionel and Mrs. Leonard, Raymond told him what a happy place he found his new home to be. He was amazed and pleased at the physical similarities between his present world and life on earth.

He related how he had first been met and welcomed warmly by his Grandfather William and then by many other relatives who seemed as real and as visibly solid as people on earth. He found them to be just as kind and loving as he had always remembered them to be.

He went on to say that he now lived in a house with trees and shrubbery and flowers about it and he was struck by the fact that his new

47

habitation and the grounds around and beyond seemed as solid and substantial as on earth. There seemed to be nothing ghostly or wispy about his new existence.

He was so fascinated with his new life that he would not want to return to earth.

In a subsequent sequence with his father and Mrs. Leonard, he spoke of how much more interesting he found life where he was than on the old earth plane. There was so much to study and learn and everything was so fascinating he wouldn't want to go back for anything in the world. He told his father he hoped he wouldn't think it selfish of him for saying that, and he also hoped he wouldn't conclude that he wanted to be away from his loved ones on earth. As a matter of fact, he said, he felt closer to them than he had ever felt before. It was all so interesting where he was that he wouldn't want to be anywhere else.

In a seance with his brother Alec and Mrs. Leonard, Raymond reported his new realm was amazingly varied and wonderfully real. Every day, he said joyfully, he was making new discoveries. He could go anywhere he wished and meet with anyone at any time - he had only to think of them and he could be with them. There were all kinds of lectures and demonstrations and other educational adventures so that opportunities for one's intellectual and spiritual development seemed to be unending.

He said he had gone to a library with his Grandfather William and found the books there to be similar to those on earth - with one extraordinary difference. There were many books there not yet published on the earth plane and many of these were much more advanced and complex than any books on earth. He was informed that the substance of some of these books - the less complex ones - would later be impressed upon the minds of receptive earthling authors and thus these books would come to earth.

He spoke of the ethical values of his new realm and of a common law of justice he found there.

Four and a half months after his departure from earth, in a seance with Lady Mary and Mrs. Leonard (Feb.4,1916), Raymond commented on the ethical values of his new realm.

There was no judge or jury on the Other Side, he told his mother. Like attracted like and you simply gravitated to where you belonged.

If you had tried to live a decent, caring life of compassion and harmlessness on earth, you were granted the privilege of living in a community of harmony and peace on the Other Side. You wound up close to those you were fond of within a fellowship of people with whom you were mentally and spiritually at home. In this felicitous, nurturing milieu you could further develop the best spiritual qualities within you.

On the other hand, the mean, the selfish and the greedy, on their graduation from the earth plane, in line with the principle that like attracts like, found themselves living with equally mean, selfish and greedy beings in an atmosphere that was a sad reflection of their own barren hearts. Here they would remain until they chose to mend their ways.

Raymond cited cases of some selfish young men whose earthly lives had been devoted to greed and vice. On the Other Side, they found themselves together with others of similar spirit in a wretched place to which Raymond said he was glad he didn't have to go. They were utterly bored and terribly unhappy with each other and with themselves in their new abode which wasn't exactly hell but was more like a reformatory. But they weren't eternally damned to stay in this hellish quarantine. All they had to do was rethink their lives and aspire to something nobler - really want it in their hearts - then they would be guided to ways to achieve such a change. In doing so, they would be assisted by more advanced souls from higher planes.

Your earthly achievements of material riches, social prestige and power were valued on the Other Side only to the extent that you had altruistically utilized these special privileges for the betterment of others. What really mattered was how humanely you had lived as an earthling, how kindly and generously you had treated others. This, as Raymond viewed it, was the paramount ethical standard of the Other Side.

He found no unfairness and no injustice in his new realm. Instead there was a common law of justice that operated equally for each and every person - and that was another reason why he loved his life on the Other Side.

He spoke of living on the third plane, of studying on higher planes, and of the opportunities for soul cultivation and spiritual development on these higher planes.

In the same seance with Lady Mary and Mrs. Leonard (Feb.4,1915), Raymond explained to his mother that there were different planes beyond the earth plane - as many as ten that he knew of - and these planes were at ascending levels of soul development.

The first two planes beyond the earth plane were for earthbound people who were not yet ready in their hearts to seek higher development. He was on the third plane - called "Summerland" or "Homeland" by many because it resembled the best and most beautiful aspects of the earth plane. He had been told he could now move up to the fourth plane whenever he chose, but he hadn't done it yet because he felt so at home where he was.

In another seance he told his parents he had been attending lectures in what they called "halls of learning" on the fifth plane. He

50

explained that you could prepare yourself for the higher planes while you were living on the lower ones.

Some of his teachers, he said, came to him from the seventh plane. These wonderful guides, who were very advanced, were teaching him how to instruct others on the lower planes about how to enlarge their horizons and begin to move upward. He was also given lessons in concentration and on the projection of illuminating thought to those on the earth plane. Having been to the fourth, fifth and sixth planes he found each one to be more beautiful and inspiring than the previous ones.

He spoke of his visit to the highest plane and of his encounter with the radiance of Christ.

In the seance previously noted Raymond told his mother in an awed voice that he had recently been escorted by his guides to visit the highest plane - a place so gorgeous it was quite indescribable - and there, unbelievable though it seemed, he had seen and heard the Christ himself!

Although he saw Him only briefly and from a distance, he called the experience the most wonderful thing that had ever happened to him. Christ was robed in shining raiment, his voice was "like a bell", but most of all, when the beautiful rays of his being shone upon him, he was thrilled and exalted beyond anything he had ever known.

Later, when he found himself back on the third plane in "Summerland," he was still so charged with his spiritual radiance that he felt he could stop rivers and move mountains and he was flooded with an all-consuming happiness.

Subsequently, he asked his guides if Christ could be seen by everyone as he had just seen him and was told that not everyone saw him in quite the same way - but that Christ was a sort of projection - something like those rays - everywhere in spirit. They added that there

51

was something of him for people on all planes including the earth plane, if they asked for his help.

He exultantly told his mother that she and his father could be sure that there *really* was a Christ, a *living Christ*, and incredible though it seemed to him, he had been allowed to see and hear this beautiful, wondrous being!

As a scientist and "evidential" researcher, Sir Oliver debated with himself whether to include this Christological incident in the chronicle of his son's life beyond death. He realized it was completely unverifiable material. He knew a number of skeptical psychologists would label it either hysterical hallucination or hopeless dementia, and certain dogma-bound churchmen would denounce it as blasphemous heresy.

Nevertheless, Sir Oliver decided he must include Raymond's personal and subjective revelation in his documentation. Regardless of what critics might say, it constituted an important benchmark in his son's portrayal of his spiritual development on the Other Side.

Those of you who are Jewish, Moslem, Buddhist or of some other non-Christian faith should understand that Raymond's earthly religious teaching, like his parents' was Church of England Protestant Christian; it was quite natural that in his initial spiritual search in the next dimension, his spirit would be drawn to the Christ of his own religious heritage.

In similar circumstances, a religious Jew might be drawn to Moses, Abraham, Isaiah or Elijah, or a Buddhist to Gautama Buddha, or a Moslem to Mohammed, in search for spiritual enlightenment. This proved to be the case in the near-death experiences discussed in CHAPTER SIX.

He offered many other comments about the quality of life in the next dimension - unverifiable, but corroborated by previous research.

Sir Oliver was inclined to accept many of Raymond's observations as credible, even though unverifiable, for one impressive reason: many previous communications of deceased earthlings were similar to Raymond's findings.

Abstracted from the dialogue of many seances, here is the essence of additional points Raymond made about his life after death:

-The feeling of love between men and women on earth continued in the next dimension.

-The closeness of families also carried over to the Other Side.

-The family bond continued to keep its members together.

-One did not eat as on earth, but was sustained by less material nourishment.

-Night did not follow day as it did on the earth plane. It seemed to become less light only when he felt like resting and this seemed to be a matter of thought.

-Communication was often accomplished soul to soul and mind to mind - not simply through words. Thus language was never a barrier.

-His body was similar to the one he had on earth, but was much lighter and much more mobile. Outwardly, he looked the same to those who knew him on earth, but he could move much more freely

and travel any place at will simply through thought.

-Soldiers he knew who had lost their limbs, or been otherwise injured in the war, were now fully restored. There were no maimed or crippled bodies, no sightless, deaf or dumb in the next realm. In death, you shed your earthly physical body and your new astral body was perfect.

-Unfortunately, there was no such sudden moral or spiritual transformation of a person's soul following his death. If your life on earth had been consecrated to material acquisitiveness, selfishness and greed, you would ultimately have to face its emptiness on the Other Side. On the other hand, if your soul had sought to grow in goodness and to perfect itself in loving and caring for others, you would happily continue that growth and development in the next realm.

-As one moved up in planes beyond the earth plane, one took on a new zest for learning, for inward development and for spiritual growth. The opportunities for such growth were fascinating, challenging and infinite in scope.

The record of these communications is in Sir Oliver's book *Raymond or Life and Death*, published in both London and New York in 1916 and in a later edition called *Raymond Revised* (1922).

*Sir Arthur Conan Doyle Reveals Some
Fascinating Answers to the Question
"What Is Life Like on the Other Side?"
Based on Forty Years of Psychic Research
Into Authentic, Documented Cases*

Most of us today remember Sir Arthur Conan Doyle chiefly for his famous Sherlock Holmes detective stories which still hold millions of readers spellbound and many more millions enthralled in movies and television. Very few of us are aware of the fact that the psychic world became the central focus of his later life.

By 1920, much to the chagrin of disbelieving friends, Sir Arthur had become an outspoken leader in the psychic realm, and perhaps the best known and most highly publicized spiritualist not only in England but throughout the world.

At this time, Sir Arthur was still a handsome, vigorous man of 61, over six feet tall, broad-shouldered and athletic in bearing. His bold, ruddy face thatched by grey-brown hair, his high cheekbones, strong jaw and searching blue eyes gave him the visage of a story-book Celtic knight. Courtly and gentle in manner, charming and friendly, he had a radiance and warmth of heart that drew people instinctively to him. He was undoubtedly one of the most beloved men of England despite the fact that critics, skeptics and even many of his admirers thought he had "gone off the deep end" on the subject of survival after death.

Overriding all criticism, he made it his personal mission throughout the twenties to remind us all that life goes on happily on the Other Side for most of our departed loved ones.

"Remember, they are not dead!" he constantly told his huge lecture hall audiences throughout Great Britain and in the major cities of Europe, the U.S.A., Canada, Australia and New Zealand, plus many parts of Africa. "None of us die! Death is not to be feared. It is simply another step in our soul's development on another plane. There is no death!"

Along with his colleague and warm friend, Sir Oliver Lodge, Sir Arthur by 1920 probably knew more about the psychic realm and the possibility of life after death than anyone living.

Yet forty years prior he had been a total disbeliever.

While he was studying medicine at the University of Edinburgh in 1880, he heard his first lecture on the subject "Does Death End It All?" by a Boston psychic. His mental response to the talk was to dismiss the idea of survival after death as purely imaginative, wishful thinking. Nevertheless, as a creative writer he found himself intrigued by the idea.

Five years later, when he set up medical practice in Southsea, England he and his first wife, Louise, attended a number of social parties which engaged in table-tilting and ouija board sessions as well as more serious seances with mediums. He remained skeptical, yet was so thoroughly captivated, that he took copious notes on all these meetings which remained in his files until the day he died.

Throughout the late eighteen-eighties and the eighteen-nineties, while he created a steady stream of best-selling Sherlock Holmes mysteries, plus a number of successful historical novels, he also continued to attend seances as a still skeptical but fascinated sleuth.

During those productive literary years, as a hobby, he avidly read all the books and articles he could find on the subject of psychic phenomena. He was impressed by the number of reputable, and even notable, witnesses who made persuasive cases for the psychic evidence of life after death. Some of them were distinguished scientists such as Sir William Crookes, the discoverer of the element thallium and inventor of the Crookes tube, the first to emit x-rays, who wrote *Psychic Force and Modern Spiritualism* (1871).

When he joined the Society for Psychical Research of Great Britain in 1891 he carefully perused its hundreds of painstakingly documented cases of psychic phenomena and stenographically transcribed communications between the living and the "dead." His skepticism wavered still more. Later he expressed his deep gratitude to the Society for its "unwearied diligence," "its sobriety of statement," and "its methodical, never-tiring work," "which now helped me to shape my thoughts."[1]

In 1900 he volunteered to serve without pay as a civilian physician for a privately-financed hospital unit which administered to the wounded and buried the dead on the South African battlefront during eight crucial months of the Boer War. Inevitably, he was stricken by the death of many of the wounded whom he could not help.

His previous quest for an answer to the world's greatest mystery had been out of scientific curiosity. Now it took on more profound importance. If only he could write with authority and conviction to the wives and parents of these young martyrs, assuring them that their brave loved ones still lived! But he was not yet sure.

When he lost his first wife, Louise, in 1906 after 21 years of congenial marriage marred only by her 13 years of illness with tuberculosis, he wrote his mother that Louise had been the most selfless, cheerful, loving person he had ever known. Now for the first time in his life the athletic, tireless, horseman, cricketeer, golfer and amateur boxer became seriously ill. He lost all zest for living, became an insomniac, suffered a terrible case of nerves, sank into deep, lethargic depression and for over six months, was a stranger to himself and to his family and friends.

Louise's death further underlined his need for an answer to the ultimate question of where one went after one's brief span on earth. Although he had known 13 years of warning, during her confinement as a tubercular invalid, that her earthly end could be the next month or even the next day, when she finally painlessly departed at 3 A.M. July 4th, 1906, at the age of 49, he could not help but ask: "Why? And where? Where now did her sweet, loving spirit go?"

He had no certain answer, but he simply *had* to believe that his dear wife's courageous, selfless spirit had to be elsewhere than buried with her lifeless body in her grave. Yet he still was not sure that his many psychic friends had the full answer to life after death.

Fourteen months later he married Jean Leckie, an enchanting woman who had been a warm friend for over a decade. An extraordinary beauty with dark golden hair, hazel green eyes, a delicate white complexion and a warm, winning smile, she also had many talents. She was a gifted singer, a lover of fine art and literature, an expert horsewoman and active sportswoman. At the same time she was deeply interested in world affairs, spiritual and religious concerns.

Sir Arthur's hundreds of literary, political and social friends were charmed by her radiance, her out-going friendliness and her keen intelligence. His mother adored her, not only because she was a fine person and her loving new daughter, but also because of the elegance and grace she brought into her son's life.

Most important of all, Jean embraced his two children - Mary Louise, then 18 and Kingsley, age 15 - as though they were her own.

Subsequently, she bore him two more sons and a second daughter - all of whom later became involved in his psychic ventures.

As their marriage unfolded, Sir Arthur and Jean discovered to their delight that they had more in common with each other than with any other person either of them had known. They were so much alike in so many ways that she seemed almost the female counterpart of his male spirit; it was a beautiful union, the close and tender love-match of two true soul-mates!

They had but one small, emotional and intellectual difference; in their early years together Jean found his psychic studies dangerous and occasionally frightening.

The Great War abruptly ended that difference. When Europe exploded into deadly combat in August of 1914, Sir Arthur was enlisted by the British government to write a history as it went on for four long years. This became an overwhelming, 16 hour-a-day assignment that took him to the front on a number of occasions and evolved into a massive, six-volume chronicle.

During those devastating war years from 1914 to 1918, all of the great nations of Europe and ultimately the United States and Canada were torn apart by the sacrificial murder of their finest young manhood - nearly 9 million killed and over 37 million wounded, with many of the wounded so cruelly maimed that death would have been more merciful. It was the most heinous slaughter of human life any war in humankind's history except World War II with over 15 million killed or missing in combat plus six million Jews and five million others destroyed by the Nazi holocaust.[2]

During that 1914-1918 period, four personally devastating events affected the spiritual and psychic lives of Sir Arthur and Jean.

In the first month of the war, Jean's brother Malcom, was killed in the battle of the Marne. At that time Jean and Sir Arthur were kindly taking care of an ailing woman in their home - a gifted psychic and automatic writer named Lily Loder-Symonds. When she contacted Malcolm after his death, Sir Arthur asked him a question about a very private conversation which they had many years prior, a conversation not even known to Jean. The details which Malcolm recalled - some long forgotten by Sir Arthur - completely convinced Sir Arthur and Jean that Malcolm still lived. As further proof, to their amazement, the automatic writing which Lily Loder-Symonds produced was in Malcolm's personal handwriting![3]

From that moment on, Jean lost all fear of the psychic and for their remaining sixteen years of marriage, she became her husband's closest partner and greatest ally in his explorations into this mysterious realm.

It was at this point that Sir Arthur put aside his role of objective explorer and joining Jean, became a committed believer in humankind's life and love after death. After 34 years of research his hard-headed mind was finally convinced that the human spirit lived on beyond this earth!

When Sir Oliver Lodge lost his beloved son, Raymond, on the battlefield of Flanders and subsequently published *Raymond or Life After Death,* Sir Arthur and Jean were deeply moved along with thousands of others who read Raymond's account of his life after death. It was then that Sir Arthur decided he must spend the rest of his life letting others know the great truth it had taken him so many years of hard study and personal anguish to discover, that there is no death!

Later he wrote about that time of decision: "From the moment that I had understood the overwhelming importance of this subject and realized how utterly it must change and chasten the whole thought of the world when it is wholeheartedly accepted, I felt...that all other work which I had ever done, or could ever do, was as nothing compared to this."[4]

From that time forward, the mission of Sir Arthur and Jean was clear. They must bring to others the solace and hope they had personally discovered beyond the abyss of hopeless grief which overwhelmed so many people when they "lost" a loved one.

That same year, 1916, Sir Arthur's oldest son, Kingsley, a captain in the 1st Hampshires, was severely wounded in the Battle of the Somme. In one of the more ghastly episodes of the Great War, 60,000 casualties were suffered and every officer in Kingsley's battalion was either wounded or killed on the first day of that engagement. Before it finally ended months later, half a million young men were lost in that long, terrible Battle of the Somme.

During the savage first twenty-four hours of action, two German bullets ripped through Kingsley's neck, but mercifully he survived. After a long hospitalization he was discharged as unfit for further combat. When the great flu epidemic swept over Europe in 1918 taking to their death hundreds of thousands, in his weakened condition, he, too, succumbed - just two weeks before the November 11th Armistice ending the war.

Only three months later, in February 1919, Sir Arthur's beloved younger brother Innes, a Brigadier General, who had somehow survived four exhausting and dangerous years of combat duty, also became a fatal casualty of the flu epidemic.

The loss of his first son and his youngest brother hit Sir Arthur very hard, but, as always, he bore his grief stoically. Again, as in the case of his brother-in-law, Malcolm, through mediums in seances he received messages which he considered verifiable evidence from both Kingsley and Innes that they still lived - which mitigated the terrible knowledge that he would never see them again on this earth.

Sir Arthur, with Jean always beside him helping in every way, began a lecture tour of all of the major communities in Great Britain. Then he took on speaking engagements in the most important cities in the United

States, Canada, Europe and Africa - everywhere speaking to record-breaking, overflow audiences.

During the next decade, Sir Arthur turned out six books on spiritualism and psychic phenomena, writing large parts of them while on shipboard, in railroad Pullman cars, and in hotel rooms while trekking the world with Jean and their three young children.

In *The Vital Message* he gave a remarkable summary of the psychic findings to date on life after death gleaned from the many seances he had personally attended and the hundreds of cases he had carefully studied either in books or in transcribed records of the British Society for Psychical Research and the London Spiritual Alliance. Nowhere, except perhaps in Sir Oliver Lodge's *Raymond or Life After Death* had life in the next dimension been more graphically described.

Here, then, based on his forty years of in-depth research are Sir Arthur's major conclusions about the quality of life in the next dimension:

1. He reported that our loved ones found themselves in a world very much like the one they had left except that everything was keyed to a higher octave.

2. They were joined by relatives and friends whom they had loved on earth and there were joyous reunions.

3. People with similar thoughts, tastes, values and feelings gravitated together. There were many happy circles of congenial people living in pleasant households with every amenity of comfort, with companionship, with domestic pets, and with art and music.

4. Most kindhearted people of good will, according to Doyle's psychic sources, found an idyllic paradise on the Other Side in a setting of inviting homes, beautiful gardens, green forests and picturesque lakes and streams.

5. Age disappeared. As our departed loved ones entered this new world, they reverted to the peak of their earthly development and the prime of their maturity.

6. "A perfect body awaits us. Such is the teaching from beyond," Doyle said. One's earthly physical body was supplanted by a perfect astral body on the Other Side. The astral body, though imperceptible to our earthly senses and of a much higher frequency, was as solid to those in the next dimension as our physical body is to us.

7. In their perfect astral bodies in their new realm, the crippled, the mutilated, the old and feeble, the sick and infirm, the birthmarked or scarred, the blind, the deaf and the dumb of our earth - all left these deficiencies behind them forever.

8. Married couples who had truly loved each other on earth continued their close union on the Other Side. Sooner or later, he said, every man and woman found a soul mate in the next realm. A person whose marriage had been parted by death more than once on earth would continue on the Other Side only with the one partner who was his or her true soul mate.

9. A child who "died" was raised to adulthood with love and care in the next world by persons who joyously assumed such responsibilities. For example, a mother who mourned the passing of her two year old baby girl, when she herself "died" 20 years later would be greeted on arrival at the Other Side by her well-trained and well-schooled 22 year old daughter.

10. Our departed loved ones carried over to the next realm their skills and abilities, their knowledge and experience, their creative gifts, their intellectual powers, their attributes of

character and their spiritual development - nothing was lost. What one learned on earth one kept for later use of increasing knowledge and spiritual growth.

11. There were no rich nor poor except in spirit in the next realm. One's riches were measured in strength of character, in selflessness, in sensitivity to others, in the capacity to love and care.

12. The idea of a merciless, grotesque hell of frightening fire and eternal damnation was refuted by Doyle's psychic sources, but they did not contradict the Biblical description of a place of "outer darkness" where there was "weeping and gnashing of teeth." The principle of like attracting like in the next world not only applied to persons of good will, but also, to those misguided beings whose earthly lives had been wasted in selfishness, in greed, in cruelty and evil. By their lives on earth they had literally condemned themselves to live in a state of quarantine with others who were their equal in selfishness, greed, cruelty and evil. Their lives in this hell of their own making would not change until they changed their values and way of life.

Unlike the higher planes which were flooded with glorious light, the atmosphere on this plane ranged from greyness to total darkness, reflecting the spirit of its various inhabitants.

No one was ever condemned to eternal perdition. The way was always open and the Light and Love from higher planes was always beckoning them to open their hearts and minds to the much more rewarding and beautiful life of higher consciousness.

13. On the whole, the Other Side was an intensely happy place for most its occupants, according to Doyle's psychic sources, and almost all expressed the view that they would not want to return to the earth plane, for life was far more exciting on the Other Side.[6]

As Sir Arthur spoke before enthralled audiences in all parts of the world, these conclusions, based on his years of research, were his fascinating answer to the one question most often asked: "what is life like on the Other Side?"

Almost as fascinating is the fact that nearly all of the evidential cases he summarized, including those of Raymond Lodge, to quote his words, *"have a remarkable though not complete similarity from whatever source they come!"*

So it would seem according to the evidence of that master sleuth, Dr. Conan Doyle, that *for most of us, our death, instead of being the desolate, abysmal end of our lives, can be - if we so choose - a joyous graduation to an exciting new world, to richer, deeper, more soul-satisfying love and to happier, more beautiful, more spiritually rewarding living on another plane!*

*World Renowned Writer Albert Payson
Terhune Returns after Death to
Reassure His Beloved Wife Anice of
His Continuing Adoration from the
Next Dimension*

Death of a loved one is not easy to accept. Even though you may firmly believe in another life after this one, the loss of a beloved one can be absolutely devastating - as though a part of your own soul has also died - as though part of your world has come to an end.

No matter how fervent your convictions about immortality are, no matter how sure your faith in life after death may be, you must face the hard fact that your loved one has physically left you - seemingly forever. Neither prayers nor the consolation and sympathy of close friends can fully alleviate the awful void of utter loneliness and the feeling of complete forsakeness that you and I and everyone experiences in those first few hours, days and weeks when a loved one has left us.

But this will pass!

Let me give you one of the most illuminating cases of life and love between this world and the next that I have ever encountered. It is a case so filled with tenderness and love that I hope it will ease your pain, inspire you and thrill you as it did me!

At the time of his passing, Albert Payson Terhune was a world renowned figure. The *Encyclopedia Britannica* carries an impressive biography which is excerpted here:

TERHUNE, ALBERT PAYSON (1872-1942) U.S.

novelist and short-story writer, famous for his popular stories about dogs, was born in Newark, N.J., on Dec. 21, 1972, the son of a Presbyterian clergyman, Edward Payson Terhune and Mary Virginia Hawes Terhune... Terhune graduated from Columbia University, New York City in 1893, traveled in Egypt and Syria, and returned to New York, joining the staff of the *New York Evening World* in 1894... He wrote assiduously in his spare time to free himself from journalism and published more than 12 books before he left the *Evening World* in 1916.

In 1919 appeared the first of his popular dog stories, *Lad, a Dog.* He had moved to a farm near Pompton Lakes, N.J., which he named "Sunnybank," and there for the rest of his life he wrote, bred prize collies, fished and hunted. He wrote more than 25 books after 1919, nearly all of them novels in which dogs play conspicuous parts, including *Bruce* (1920), *The Heart of a Dog* (1925), *Lad of Sunnybank* (1928) and *A Book of Famous Dogs* (1937). He also wrote two autobiographical books, *Now that I'm Fifty* (1925) and *To the Best of My Memory* (1930). He died at Sunnybank on February 18th, 1942.[1]

It should be added that Terhune's universally loved stories about collie dogs reached millions of readers in the United States and other English-speaking countries and through translations, many more millions all over Europe and South America. A series of Hollywood movies and a smash-hit television series focusing on "Lassie" brought his stories to additional millions of movie-goers and televiewers all over the world.

Bert was a giant of a man - 6 feet three and a half inches in height, a handsome, life-loving person who reveled in outdoor living, hunting and fishing; at the same time he appreciated the symphony and opera, the ballet and theater. He found great pleasure in the camaraderie of his journalist friends and fellow members of the Explorers Club, the Adventurers Club, the Lambs Club, the Players Club and the Century Club in New York City. He also treasured the tranquility of his later years of sanctuary on Sunnybank farm - but above all he loved his adoring wife and the exciting life they enjoyed together.

Anice or "Annie" as he fondly called her, was a perfect mate for Bert, an enchanting lady who kept a gracious home for him while at the same time pursuing her own creative talents as writer, poet, composer and musician.

Bert and Anice had been childhood sweethearts from grade school days in Springfield, Massachusetts and were married soon after his graduation from Columbia University. They were drawn to each other from the moment they first met as though they had been soul-mates in some previous existence. In their early married life they experienced some physical hardship and financial struggle during the time Bert was proving himself as a reporter for the *New York Evening World,* but their love life and marriage always remained an intimate, devoted partnership.

As a journalist for the *World,* Bert was tireless, versatile, innovative and prolific. During his 22 years with the venerable metropolitan newspaper, he wrote every sort of story from human interest and sporting features to dramatic criticism to a daily personally by-lined column. He was, in a sense, the *Evening World's* superwriter. There was seemingly no limit to his talents.

He wrote a series of fascinating historical feature articles on such themes as "Fifty Famous Wars," "Fifty Failures Who Made Good," "Fifty

Famous Fakes," "Stories of Our Country," etc., that proved so popular they ran daily in the *Evening World* for *over ten years!*

When his editors needed someone to ghost-write an article for Lillian Russell, the famed eighteen-nineties beauty, singer and lady friend of "Diamond Jim" Brady, Bert got the job. Aided by his darling Anice as both reader and reviewer, he wrote a regular "Book Column," reviewing the latest, most interesting books .

He and Anice saw many of the Metropolitan's opera productions and most of Broadway's new plays; in exchange for two choice seats on the aisle on opening nights, he turned out reviews for the next day's editions of the *World*.

As a reporter, his writing was always straight-forward, fast moving and sparkling with excitement. When he was hard up for a story, he went out and found one. Having been a skilled boxer during his college years, he suggested to his editor that he box three rounds with six of the greatest professional prizefighters - James Corbett, Jim Jeffries, Bob Fitzsimmons, Tom Sharkey, Gus Ruhlin and Kid McCoy and write features about each of these encounters.

Amazed at Bert's audacity, his editor enthusiastically endorsed the idea, but as a practical joke, unknown to Bert, privately promised each of the star prizefighters lots of free advertising in the *World* if he could knock Bert out! Some joke!

But the joke was on the editor. Although Bert wound up with a bruised hand from one fight, a cut lip for another and a black eye from a third encounter, not one of the six champions could knock him out or even knock him down. World heavyweight champion Jim Corbett, after his three rounds with Bert, called him "the best amateur boxer in America!"

Needless to say, Bert's stories about these fights sold countless newspapers and earned him many avid readers.

On the side, as a free-lancer, Bert pounded out swashbuckling serials and adventure yarns which regularly appeared in *Argosy, Cosmopolitan, Redbook* and other popular magazines and were subsequently published as full-length books.

At the request of David Belasco, the theater genius, Bert took his play, *The Return of Peter Grimm,* a fascinating drama about a dead man's return to life, and rewrote it as a novel.

At age 44, his free-lance writing had proven to be so successful he was able to give up his *Evening World* job, much to his editor's fervent regret. Who could possibly fill Bert Terhune's unique place? For two years thereafter, they kept his name on the editorial masthead in hope he might return.

Bert was not to return - ever.

It all started when Ray Long, the editor of the popular monthly magazine, *Redbook,* visiting the Terhunes at "Sunnybank," suggested to Bert that he should write a story about his prize collie, Lad. At first Bert dismissed the idea. He had always thought that what the public wanted was romantic stories - "he and she stuff," as he put it.

As Long persisted, Bert listened hard and then wrote his first story about Lad. Because of its success many more followed, published in *Redbook, Cosmopolitan,* and *The Saturday Evening Post.* In 1919 the stories were put together in an E. P. Dutton book, *Lad, a Dog* which took the country by storm and completely changed the lives of Bert and Anice. Anice attributed Bert's fame almost entirely to "dear old Laddie." From that year forward, Bert never again had financial worries.

For the next twelve years, from 1916 when he left the *Evening World* until 1928, their life together became more bountiful, joyous and adventurous than ever. Anice blissfully called it, "the golden sunshine of the high noon of our lives!"

71

Eight months of each year they spent at Sunnybank. It was no longer simply a vacation home and weekend retreat but the center for all their creative activities. The winter months of the year they went back to their New York City apartment to enjoy the opera, symphonies and a happy whirl of social activities with dear friends.

During these years Bert's literary output was prodigious. His many magazine stories were gathered into some 20 books which were not only U.S. bestsellers, but also, having been translated, enjoyed a vast foreign readership.

At the same time, Anice composed quantities of music for the famous United States music publishing house, G. Schirmer, Inc. Also, she contributed verse, stories and articles for *The Ladies Home Journal, McClure's, Good Housekeeping,* and *The Atlantic Monthly.* She, too, produced books, 17 of them by that time, three of them novels, several on music and a number of them books of songs for children and ballads for young people.

During these golden years, they made joyous treks to such places as London and England, Dublin and Ireland, Edinburgh and Scotland, Paris, Nice and Monte Carlo in France, Madrid and Barcelona in Spain, Rome, Naples, Florence, Venice and other cities in Italy, Mexico City and Mexico, Cairo and Egypt, Jerusalem and Haifa and other areas of the Holyland, as well as long sojourns to Florida and San Francisco and northern California.

Their social life at Sunnybank and in New York City was rich in brilliant conversation and warm friendship. Their guests ranged from the novelist, Sinclair Lewis and the Arctic explorer, Dr. Vilhjalmur Stefansson, to Bert's motley crew of newspaper friends, to producers, actors, directors and playwrights of the Lambs Club and the Players Club. Their friends included world travelers, archaeologists, geographers and other scientists of the Explorers Club to distinguished writers and editors of the Authors

Club, to eminent statesmen, industrialists, scholars, educators, artists, writers and clergymen of the Century Club.

Many of these warm friends gathered at Sunnybank for two special events what meant much to Bert and Anice - the gala wedding reception of their daughter, Lorraine, in June 1923 - and the celebration of their Silver Wedding Anniversary September 2nd, 1928, when over 350 of their admirers paid them loving tribute for their quarter of a century of nearly perfect marriage.

These were happy years, productive years of tender comradeship - described by Anice in his biography, *The Bert Terhune I Knew,* written after his death, as the most idyllic chapter of their lives. She called that chapter, "The Top of the Hill."

Then, suddenly, seemingly without reason or meaning, tragedy struck their lives.

Late in the evening of December 13, 1928, Bert was having a problem with the serial on which he was working. As he often did when trying to unravel a snag in his writing, he took a short walk on one of the little-traveled roads about Sunnybank Farm.

Suddenly, he was struck by a hit-and-run driver speeding at a mad rate on the wrong side of the road. The impact of the car colliding with his body threw him high into the air and landed him in bushes several yards off the road - completely unconscious.

When consciousness returned, he managed to drag his injured body to the road and flagged down another more friendly driver who helped him get back to Sunnybank. Anice, deeply worried because he had been gone so long, was aghast at the bleeding, mauled sight of him. But thank God, he was alive!

Immediately dispatched to the nearest hospital, his many broken bones and internal injuries were properly treated. He was in bed for weeks and on crutches for many more, but never fully recovered from the physical damage of the accident. In constant pain for the rest of his life, he was periodically in and out of hospitals for operations, each time coming out a little weaker.

Determined to get well because of his deep love for Anice, he bore his pains without complaint. He treasured the life they had and wanted many more years of it.

He graduated from crutches to a cane and continued to write, though not as prolifically. The long, exhilarating walks he and Anice used to enjoy were no longer possible. The stimulating world travels in which they had reveled had to be cut back to short trips to New York, brief excursions to Washington, D.C. and an ocean cruise to London. Their lives became quieter, more subdued, more an inward adventure.

Both Bert and Anice were deeply religious and during this period he undertook to write a book he considered the highlight of his creative life - series of essays on Jesus entitled *The Son of God.* Futilely fighting to regain full health, he hammered out an autobiography, *To the Best of My Memory.*

Despite the weakened condition of his body, he found a new talent - he became a popular radio raconteur. His beautiful voice and natural gift for story telling made him a star performer.

Despite his valiant efforts, his health continued to fail. On the eve of his 69th birthday, December 21st, 1941, Anice brought him home after his latest - and last operation. As they trimmed their 41st Christmas tree, he told Anice, "I don't know how anyone could be as happy as we are!" Yet he knew his earthly life was drawing to a close. So did Anice, but she was not ready face the fact.

In late February, a few days before his passing, knowing that he was going, he said to Anice softly, but firmly, "I shall come back. I shall be here at Sunnybank with you, I promise."

On February 21st, 1942, with her arms around him, he peacefully moved to the next dimension.

In his inimitable way Bert had tried to prepare Anice for his bodily parting. Many months prior to his demise, they had discussed an article he had planned to write entitled "Across the Line." In that article he had hoped to offer reassurance to those who grieved for the loss of their loved ones. At the same time he hoped that these thoughts might one day in her hour of need give comfort to Anice.

Bert's notes raised a number of fundamental questions we all have about death. He asked, for example, what happened to a person after he "crossed the line," as he put it. His body - his shell - was buried, and after some chemical changes, that shell became part of the earth. But what became of his vigor and his motive power and that something some people call a soul? What happened to his laughter, his ideals, his aspirations? Were they just a part of that shell? And buried with it? He felt that if life was not a school and if we were not put here by some Higher Power for some purpose, then life was just a cruel joke.

This he could not believe.

He was positive, instead, that there were Divine answers to these profound questions.

He was sure that the opportunities for growth and development that we experienced on earth did not end with socalled "death." He was certain that there was a personal and real future life for everyone of us - and that the insights and love learned in this life would carry forward into the next dimension. He based this rock-solid faith not only on logic and common sense but on these key words from the New Testament:

75

"'In my Father's house are many mansions'... 'Behold I go to prepare a place for you'... 'This day shalt thou sup with me in Paradise'... 'Blessed are the dead which die in the Lord.'... 'He that cometh unto Me, though he were dead, yet shall he live.'"[2]

To find some of the answers to his keen-minded questions, it was first necessary that Bert himself pass through the experience of dying. After that passage to the other side, it was some time before he was able to reach back across the void to communicate with Anice.

The house that was so warm and delightful when he was there was now cold and aloof. The gardens and countryside about the house which were so beautiful and inviting when they viewed them together were grey and forbidding without him beside her.

She had expected him to be with her immediately, but this was not so. He was just gone, utterly gone!

Nevertheless, after days of utter loneliness something happened. With no special preludes, somehow an exultant feeling swept over her that she was no longer alone, that Bert was there! She just *knew* he was there!

It was as though the black gloom shrouding her had abruptly lifted. She sensed his loving presence in the room with her and felt flooded with happiness. Knowing he was there made all the difference!

Now she could go on with all the fretful business details concerning his death, the legal conferences regarding the settling of his estate and the often frustrating search for needed records and documents that had been buried in a sea of papers on his desk for over a year.

A few days after this sensing his presence, the American Kennel Club wrote asking for the names and pedigrees of every one of their

76

collies. A man whose puppy had been sired by one of their prize-winning dogs was also pressuring her for a pedigree so he could register the pup with the Kennel Club.

Pedigrees, like most of the business details of breeding prize-winning collies, running their farm and handling the finances of their writing arrangements with various publishers, had been Bert's province. Bert had always felt she had more than enough to do running their gracious home, entertaining their many guests, caring for their daily meals and many other personal needs, along with her writing and composing. But now this burden was hers.

She searched high and low for the pedigrees of their dogs and a form to fill out for the gentleman who had asked for it, but nowhere could she find them. Every bureau and desk drawer in his study and all over the house was pulled out and searched, every pile of papers scanned. But there was no sign of the precious documents.

After the third attempt, in spite of herself, tears filled her eyes. Why, oh why, dear God, was she left alone to do this hopeless job? Feeling utterly useless, against her will she broke down and sobbed in sheer frustration.

Just then, she heard Bert's voice in her mind, speaking to her as clearly as though he were there. Calmly, he said, *"Look behind you. The papers you want are right behind you."*

She swung around and her hand went out to an inconspicuous knob of a little drawer in a nest of drawers. She'd looked there before, but this time she pulled out all the papers. Underneath all the papers were the pedigrees of all of their dogs.

It was now clear that her dear Bert was keeping his promises; he was not only beside her, but helping her!

Even if she could not see him, she could feel his nearness and sense his help.

The next real manifestation came on Maundy Thursday evening when she went to church with a neighbor.

On a forbidding, stormy evening as she sat in church her thoughts went out to Bert buried in the churchyard. Overwhelmed with despair at his loss, she began to cry, pulling down the veil of her hat to hide her blinding tears from the eyes of the people about her.

Suddenly her head jerked up and she saw two lights moving quickly about on the ceiling of the church. She wondered if they might be signal lights from passing busses. Then one light disappeared and the other came closer to her, throwing a soft radiance. Then out of that radiance appeared the image of Bert, as real as life, above her and in front of her about twelve feet away. From his quiet eyes the message came through: he was not out there in the churchyard. He was right there with her, more alive than ever before! And he would be with her always!

With gentle insistence he put this message into her mind. She was thrilled and overwhelmed with happiness at the thought that although he came to her from another world, he seemed the same as he had always been, the same, dear, wonderful Bert!

She said nothing to anyone about what she had seen.

On her way home, she asked her neighbor if she had noticed any strange lights during the service, and her neighbor replied, "No, nothing except the candles."

Three weeks later she asked her minister if he had seen anything unusual during the Maundy Thursday service.

He shook his head saying, "No, I saw nothing. But I am sure you saw something. Your face was so radiant, you must have been seeing a vision!"

In the following days sensing Bert's tender vibrations on many occasions, she thought more and more about their forty beautiful years together. The idea came to her that it would be appropriate to write a book about that glorious partnership. *The Bert Terhune I Knew* seemed to write itself and in the writing she seemed closer to him than ever before. With the completion of the book she asked herself expectantly, with wonder and awe: what next?

She did not have to wait long for an answer. Only a few days later she received a letter from a stranger. This person said she was writing at the suggestion of a mutual friend. Although she was not a professional psychic medium, through automatic writing she was sometimes able to contact persons who had departed from this earth and were now in the next dimension. She understood Anice had lost her husband and she would be glad to try to get word from him or about him through her contacts on the Other Side.

She wanted no money for doing this and warned Anice that she could not promise any results; indeed, she said, nothing might come of their meeting. Nevertheless, if Anice thought it would be helpful, she offered to come to Sunnybank to visit with her and try to make contact.

At first, Anice was wary. Even though she knew of some gifted and truly sensitive mediums who had helped many people, she was also well aware that the psychic field had more than its share of money-grubbing charlatans who made their livelihood preying on people who were stricken with grief. The last person she wanted to be involved with at this time in her life was a mercenary, psychic faker.

To check out this stranger, she called their mutual acquaintance. The friend responded enthusiastically, explaining that the lady who had written to Anice was a beautiful person, a really gifted psychic whom she felt might be able to help Anice in this difficult time.

Anice arranged for Mrs. S___ to come to lunch at Sunnybank. After a pleasant repast on the veranda, Mrs. S___, a beautiful and charming person, took paper and pencil in hand and waited for someone to move her hand in automatic writing, again cautioning Anice that nothing might happen. She sat in the hammock, relaxed, blanking out her mind for whatever message might come. Anice sat on a low chair nearby, quietly, hopefully, waiting for a response.

Presently the pencil in Mrs. S___'s hand began to move across her paper and when she reached the bottom of the page she passed the sheet to Anice with her left hand while continuing with her right.

Anice looked down and was astounded.

A clear message had come through!

From Bert himself!

Here is the essence of what he wrote, using the hand of Mrs. S___.

He was cured of his ills. He now felt well and strong. He was right there on the porch with Mrs. S___ and her at that very moment.

He urged Anice to listen for his voice for he would later send messages directly to her mind. He called their exchange of thoughts a curious embodiment of electrical force which he compared to radio communication but of a vastly finer power - a positive, powerful electrical force.

He assured her that he was now with her as he had always been, that their lives would be reknitted, that they would later be united and go on their happy way together, and that their love would endure forever.

Her eyes filled up as she read what he had written. Then Mrs. S___'s hand moved again. *He begged her not to cry.*

This amazed Anice - for it meant he had actually seen her tears!

In closing, *he sent his love but was loath to end his letter because it brought them closer together. Then he signed it "love - adieu - Bert."*

Mrs. S___ did not know Bert, had never read his books nor heard him speak. Yet, according to Anice, the language was unmistakably Bert's. The words "of vastly finer power" and the statement that their lives would be reknitted were exactly the way Bert expressed himself! When she started to cry out of happiness on reading the first page of his letter, his admonition not to cry out came immediately in automatic writing, proving conclusively to Anice that Bert was right there and could see her and hear her even if she as an earthling could not see or hear him.

Both Anice and Mrs. S___ were overwhelmed. Neither of them had expected such an inspiring and evidential response. She said his letter was to both of them like a bolt of lightning out of a blue sky.

Four more letters from Bert through Mrs. S___'s automatic writing followed. Here are some highlights of what he wrote:

In his second letter, several days later, he said coming across the line was just the same as awakening on any day, but to a much different picture. Since that time he had met many old friends who had "died" in recent years, yet now were well and in the prime of their lives.

Two weeks later he told Anice that all he asked for now was that their love would continue, brightened by the contact he was now making with her. He felt it was no accident that Mrs. S___ had come to Sunnybank to bring them together and expressed the belief that her coming had been planned. He said that her coming showed that in the great Plan of Life, he and Anice - and other people like them - were not forgotten and that despite the vastness of that great Plan, were nevertheless a part of the Plan.

In the fourth letter, Bert pressed on to reassure her of the reality of his survival and of their unchanging, eternal love. He was sure the best years were yet to come. He said he would try to pass the time in useful work until she joined him and prayed the intervening years would not be too lonely for her.

He told her he was now with his parents and said that they rejoiced in his visits with their dear daughter-in-law through Mrs. S___. He relayed their love to her and promised that they, too, would one day write her a letter.

At the close of the fourth letter he expressed his gratitude to Mrs. S___ for all her kindness and thoughtfulness and then wrote to Anice, *"You, sweetheart, I kiss goodnight."*

Much to her amazement, the next communication Anice took down herself - her first experience in automatic writing! Never before had she tried to do automatic writing, but while resting on the veranda about to read a book, a voice in her head kept insisting, *"Get a pencil! Go get a pencil and paper right away!"*

She tried to ignore the voice and opened up her book but the voice gave her no peace. She went inside the house, picked up a tablet and pencil, then came back and settled down in her chair with the tablet across her lap and the pencil in her hand resting on it. For several minutes she waited - wondering - hoping - praying for a message from her dear Bert.

Suddenly she found herself writing - writing swiftly and surely - but it was not her personal handwriting and it was not her own thought - it was a message from the Other Side!

Perhaps from Bert!

To her astonishment, it was not from him. It was from her father-in-law, the Reverend Dr. Terhune. He addressed her as *"Annie, my darling"* and reported how well Bert was doing in his new life of the spirit. He said that he and Mary (Bert's mother) were with their son now to help him, and they had been trying their best to help her too.

He confessed that he and Bert had visited her on Maundy Thursday evening because she seemed so desperately in need of help. He and Bert both felt they had to let her know they were alive and with her for a moment in time there in that church (Anice deducted that her father-in-law Edward must have been that second light she saw). He went on to say how pleased he was to observe that his darling Anice had been much happier since that Maundy Thursday.

He told her how well prepared Bert was for the new life he was leading and how proud she should be of him. He expressed his gratitude to her for her great help to Bert during his life on earth, and said it was her firm faith along with Bert's own that had prepared him so well for his life on the Other Side. He now marveled at his son's goodness and sweetness and noted that his gentleness and loving kindness had paved the way for him and won a high place for him. He said he admired Bert even more than he had before,

He counseled her to keep her heart strong and keep it light and assured her she had nothing to fear now or in the future - for Bert would be waiting for her until Almighty God granted her permission to join her husband - and then happiness would be boundless - and forever. Even now, he told her, they were not really separated - their tie was very close.

He ended with the benediction of his faith:

The Lord bless you and keep you. The Lord make his face to shine upon you and give you peace, from this time forth and even forevermore. Amen.

Anice had known her beloved father-in-law for only seven years before his death but she had grown to love him as though he was truly her own father and he felt the same about her.

She was thrilled to have received this letter. She was even more thrilled to discover she had the capacity to serve as a medium through automatic writing. This meant that without the help of a third person, she could regularly be in contact with her beloved Bert.

Anice became a readily tuned-in receiving station of Bert's immediate thoughts and feelings while she, in turn, responded to him directly in speech or thought, but usually simply through thought.

Sometimes she would acutely sense Bert's presence and pick up her pencil and pad and let him speak through her writing. At other times, she would quietly call to him in her thoughts, and after a few moments he would come to her in mind-to-mind communication.

Mindful of Bert's notes for a projected article "Across the Line," which they had discussed at great length prior to his departure, Anice asked her mate a host of questions, questions all of us have asked in wonder and hope about what we might expect beyond the horizons of our earth-bound lives.

When Anice asked Bert to tell her more about his new world, he answered that life on his side was so beautiful and so enchanting that it was impossible for him to adequately describe it.

In his new life he found an intensity of thought, of mind and of perception - and a great expansion of power - and of love and beauty in all directions. He described life there as much like life on earth only intensified a hundredfold. Flowers, trees, animals, birds and above all, people seemed more radiantly beautiful. He compared life there to Shangri-La only far more beautiful and wonderful.

Anice wanted to know all about his parents whom she loved deeply. It was a thrilling surprise to see them and be with them, Bert answered. He said they were just the same as ever only more so - so happy together, thoughtful and sweet to each other. They were not old now but in what he called the best of middle life, the prime of their lives.

He described how they greeted him when he awakened from his sleep after death at Sunnybank. They were there with him immediately before and after his death in the bedroom he and Anice shared - and when he awakened from death, they put their arms around him and his mother kissed him - and then they brought him home to his present abode on the Other Side.

He told her his father helped many newly arrived souls as he had helped them. His mother was helping bring up those children who were called upon to leave their earthly home while still undeveloped - she was helping in their upbringing and development and she loved her work.

He found joy in comradeship with warm friends who were kindred in spirit.

He told her many of their old friends were there with him and they were having happy times as in former years. He longed for her to be a part of these fascinating conversations.

He explained intimate details of his new life: exquisite music, literature, the "real" Sunnybank waiting for Anice, his "shining raiment."

Since she was a skilled musician and gifted composer, she naturally wanted to know about music. He said the music on his plane was more wonderfully beautiful than any music one hears on earth and went on to say that all of the really good music originated from the Other Side and was sent down to earth composers to use as they saw fit.

The same was true, he said, of books and literature, of painting and sculpture, of architecture and other art forms. The thoughts that comprise these creative works of art were sent to receptive souls on earth who were open to them.

She wanted to know if he read books and he answered, "Yes, certainly." He reported that there was every sort of good literature where he was - not only earth books but books created at different planes of human development far beyond his present plane.

Curious about his house, she wondered what was in it. He told her that it had everything that she as a gracious homemaker, could wish for including, he boasted, the most beautiful piano and organ in the universe.

As one who had always looked after Bert's wardrobe, Anice couldn't resist asking him about what kind of apparel he wore on his present plane.

After a protracted silence, he slowly wrote that one might call it a robe of a sort. Then he noted that the Bible said that those of the spirit were clothed *"in shining raiment."* That, he said, was about the best explanation he could give her.

He spoke of rest without night, of "sustenance from the frequency," of "God's love working through and around us," and travel by "ether-transport, thought-propelled."

He told her that was no night on the Other Side, but there was rest for the soul.

When she asked how he rested, he replied quite simply that he got *"sustenance from the frequency"* and went on to explain that the River of God flowed from the Godhead through all of the different planes of the universe and was the Water of Life. When he bathed in it, that was all he needed. He said that during those precious times one was alone with one's Maker, the Light was softly restful, a beatific feeling permeated the soul and he came away infused with new energy and strength.

Then Anice wanted to know what a house was for - since they didn't rest or sleep in it. A house was simply a place to enjoy, he answered, a place where they refreshed themselves in a pleasant community of thought by listening to and taking part in conversations on every subject imaginable. A house was a family and community center.

Tirelessly she pressed on for more and more information. She wanted to know where he was when she called him since he so often immediately responded. He told her that wherever she was, he was only just beyond the horizon and wherever he was, he could always hear her and would always come to her.

"But how do you get to me," she wanted to know - "how do you travel?"

His answer was simple, but profound: *"by ether transport, thought-propelled!"*

He explained his work of welcoming newcomers
and helping "those who wish to be helped."

Among his varied assignments, he helped others following their earthly "death" as he had been helped by his parents when they led him to the Other Side. He found it a beautiful and satisfying duty to be able to give a helping hand to those who wished to be assisted. It was a joy to assure them that they could readily find happiness in this new domain.

Sometimes he was asked to bring the little children, who had been destined to leave earth prematurely, to a place where they would grow up and become happy and useful and acquire an education. There were special teachers to guide them and one of them was his mother Mary who had a special gift with children. She taught them to grow up into supremely valuable personalities.

87

He was often sent on terrestrial missions to bring
"dead" servicemen "across the line."

One day, when she asked him what he had been doing that day, she got an answer that further clarified one of his various duties.

Bert answered that he'd been on a "terrestrial journey." He went on to explain that it was sometimes his duty to escort to the next dimension young soldiers who had been killed in battle (this was 1943 - the height of World War II).

More often than not, these youthful martyrs who had met death suddenly had no idea of what had happened to them.

He felt deep compassion for them as they tried to reconcile themselves to the fact of their "death" and the reality of their present condition and whereabouts. Some were fearful, some angry and defiant and some so confused they still wanted to go on fighting. Most were simply surprised and grateful that they were still alive and bewildered as to what to do next.

It was part of Bert's job to explain their next steps; he said it was a glorious feeling to escort those who were ready in their hearts and minds to move on to a higher plane. For there, "for all who wished to obey God's will," they would find happiness and beauty beyond anything they had ever known on earth!

He found the religion of the Other Side was love
and service, and the major concern "the care and
cultivation of the soul."

She asked about religion and he responded with simplicity that religion where he was meant *love* and *service*. It was as simple and as profound as that. Dogma had nothing to do with it. The whole of religion was in Christ's teachings of love and service. Whenever help was asked, one's prayers were always heard and answered - though not always in the way one expected.

He humbly told Anice how his teacher came down from the tenth plane to help him in his studies toward enlightenment. In awe he said that his teacher had the wisdom of the ages and he revered him more than words could express.

He spoke of planes of spiritual development.

The first two planes were where newcomers arrived, and then, in accordance with one's spiritual development and the selflessness and substance of one's soul, the individual would move to more advanced planes.

Shortly after his arrival Bert found himself on the sixth plane where his parents came down from the seventh to be with him. Presumably, one could readily move from plane to plane as well as from plane to earth and back again.

At one point, Bert said he had been assigned to bring newly-arrived souls from the lower planes to higher ones more in tune with their own spiritual development; he mentioned how tired this assignment sometimes made him.

She asked him why this assignment was so wearying. He explained that the two lowest planes were where the defiant, embittered or angry souls resided until they became reconciled. It was his task to try to raise their horizons and persuade them to seek higher levels of consciousness. Unfortunately, he was not always successful.

The tenth plane was the highest known to him at that time; after that only God knew what was in store for the advancing soul. This was what he found so bewilderingly wonderful about the Other Side - no matter what one's stage of development was, every human being could, step by step, take advantage of infinite opportunities to expand their consciousness and increase their capacity for love through understanding and selfless service. But the choice was always up to each individual to decide whether - and at what pace - he or she chose to develop - if at all.

He gave her insights into their previous incarnations together.

As they discussed spiritual progress, Anice asked what he had learned on the Other Side about humankind's beginnings.

He said that he and Anice, like everyone else, first began as elementary atoms, then eons later knew life as human beings. Years and years ago they had driven donkeys in the market places of Abyssinia, they had roamed the streets of Baghdad selling flowers, they were in Greece, in Spain, in England and elsewhere - they both had experienced many different incarnations and they were always together.

He said he had been allowed to read the Akashic Records - the Book of Life - which traced humankind's history from the beginning of time. He went on to say how amazing it was to view the progress of the human soul from its simple beginnings. One could not help but feel elation after viewing humankind's gradual progress from its rudimentary roots.

I'm sure you're wondering - as I did when I first encountered the phrase - what Bert meant by Akashic Records. The best explanation I have found comes from the psychic genius Edgar Cayce. In *Many Mansions - the Edgar Cayce Story on Reincarnation,* Gina Cerminara's outstanding book about "the sleeping prophet," she interprets the Akashic Records as follows:

Akasha is a Sanskrit word that refers to the fundamental etheric substance of the universe, electro-spiritual in composition. Upon this Akasha there remains impressed an indelible record of every sound, light, movement or thought since the beginning of the manifest universe. The existence of this record accounts for the ability of the clairvoyants and seers to literally see the past, no matter how remote it may be and no matter how inaccessible to ordinary human knowledge. Akasha registers impressions like a sensitive plate, and can almost be regarded as a huge candid-camera of the cosmos. The ability to read these vibratory records lies inherent within each of us, dependent upon the sensitivity of our organization, and consists in attuning to a proper degree of consciousness - much like tuning a radio to the proper wave-length.

To put it simply, Bert had been reading from an incredible tapestry of history preserved in some unknown dimension of our vast universe. The renowned Swiss psycho-therapist Dr. Carl G. Jung has referred to a similar phenomenon as "the collective unconscious."

He offered her a vision of their ultimate spiritual development.

He said they had been brought thus far through their love for each other and through God's Love and Light which surrounds and envelopes the whole universe. Merging their individuality and united in mind and spirit, they would work as one from higher planes for peace and harmony. He wistfully noted that if earthlings could but see the beauty and the glory of the Other Side and its infinite possibilities, grief would be banished forever.

He thought of Anice constantly "in the midst of all these wonders" and expressed his everlasting love in each communication. He rejoiced with her in the miracle of their love for one another and in the tenderness, beauty and ecstacy of their daily communion.

He told her they must not dwell upon their separation but should rejoice instead on their beautiful communion which was a gift from God for which they should be eternally grateful.

Bert had always had a great interest in Anice's writing as well as her other creative activities.

Her book, *The Bert Terhune I Knew,* had already been written and sent off to the publishers before Bert first communicated to her through automatic writing. Now there was another book Bert wanted her to write, a book that would assure all his friends and many others that life went on after socalled "death."

As Bert talked to her about this new book, she recalled the many profound questions he had asked in his notes for his unwritten article "Across the Line" and she gradually began to realize that he had already answered most of those questions in his dialogue with her.

She had received her first letter from Bert without outside help August 5, 1942, and during the next two and one-half months, they were in almost daily conversation. Suddenly, on October 17 at the close of one of his daily communications, he wrote: *"Darling, our book is written!"* And then he said a prayer that the book would have God's blessing and would be a message of hope and certainty to all those who read it!

The book, of course, had not as yet been actually written. What Bert was saying to his beloved Anice in essence was, "All right, dear

Annie, I've given you the answers as best I can from where I'm at. Now *you* put it all together and make a book out of it."

Which was exactly what she did!

Under his guidance she put together a small book that began with his short essay and notes on what he hoped might happen to all of us "across the line." This was followed by her narration of all that transpired after he came to her following his death.

The book, entitled not surprisingly, *Across the Line,* was published in 1945 by E. P. Dutton and Company, the house which had first published the book which had changed their lives - the best seller, *Lad, a Dog.*

It was hailed by Dr. Sherwood Eddy, a distinguished clergyman and missionary, and author of over thirty popular books including a splendid treatise on *You Will Survive After Death*, as: "most clear, convincing and helpful...It shows unmistakably, I think, satisfying evidence of the survival of individual personality...This book will give to many just the grounds for faith and hope they need."

The Reverend Dr. Joseph R. Sizoo, President of the New Brunswick (N.J.) Theological Seminary, who wrote a Foreword for the book commented: "The human heart has always rebelled against the silence of death...Here is the record of one who makes the great affirmation that it is not only possible but that it has been experienced. This is not the first voice that has protested against the silence of death and cried out exultantly, 'I have heard and I have seen.' Read it, good friend, thoughtfully, hopefully and prayerfully. When you do, new meaning will come to the ageless confession of the Christian faith, 'I believe in the communion of saints.'"

CHAPTER FIVE

*Britain's Top Aviator, Capt. Hinchliffe,
Only Days after His Fatal Trans-Atlantic
Crash, Lovingly Looks after His Wife and
Small Children from the World Beyond,
Later Gives a Graphic Picture of His
Meaningful Life on the Other Side.*

March 13, 1928 at 8:35 A.M. Britain's leading aviator, Capt. Walter Raymond Hinchliffe, took off in a Stinson monoplane from the R. A. F. aerodrome at Cranwell in an attempt to make the first non-stop, east-west crossing of the Atlantic Ocean from Great Britain to New York. Five hours later, his single-engine plane was spotted over Cork County, Ireland, then disappeared into the ominous grey clouds over the Atlantic Ocean, never to be seen or heard from again.

Eighteen days later while awaiting a communication through her ouija board from her beloved son who was killed in World War I, Mrs. Beatrice Earl was interrupted by an urgent message from a discarnate person who claimed to be the missing Capt. Hinchliffe.

An amateur student of psychical phenomena, Mrs. Earl made no claim to being a medium but had considerable psychic skill and had been comforted over the years by the happy and heartening messages she had received from her deceased son. The tone of Hinchliffe's messages was quite different; it was so urgent it was almost frantic. He begged Mrs. Earl to get in touch with his wife and in subsequent messages, told her she could reach his wife through his solicitor, even spelling out the solicitor's name, DRUMMONDS - and the street and town where he was located - HIGH STREET, CROWDON. Much to her surprise, such a solicitor's name at that address was indeed listed in the phone book.

On April 12, because of the emotional urgency expressed in his messages and because he had implored her on two more occasions to get in touch with his wife, Mrs. Earl decided to take the risk and relay his messages to Mrs. Hinchliffe. Fearful, however, that her letter might be dismissed as the product of a deranged mind or the twisted brainstorm of a "quack" or a "crank," she also wrote to Sir Arthur Conan Doyle, seeking his counsel.

On receipt of her letter, gallant Sir Arthur immediately moved to assist her. First, he sleuthed out the name of Hinchliffe's solicitor and found it coincided with the name and address given by Mrs. Earl. He wrote Mrs. Hinchliffe an encouraging letter in which he expressed deep sympathy for her grief. He told her "Mrs. Earl has what looks like a true message from your husband, sending his love and assurance that all is well with him." He observed that the fact her husband's solicitor's address was correct "is surely notable."

As a consequence of Sir Arthur's thoughtful letter, Mrs. Hinchliffe became a trusting friend of Mrs. Earl who in turn put her in touch with the now world famous trance medium, Eileen Garrett. Mrs. Garrett had become noted for the accuracy of her information from persons on the Other Side.

In the course of a number of seances Mrs. Hinchliffe subsequently had with this incredibly gifted medium, her husband, Capt. Hinchliffe, convinced his wife that he still existed, proving to her by many personal and intimate, evidential remarks that he was very much alive, albeit in another dimension. Secondly, he gave her wise counsel to insure his family's financial security in a way that amazed her.

Thirdly, in much later seances, he gave a moving and graphic picture of his life on the Other Side.

Several months later, Mrs. Hinchliffe was so moved by these seemingly miraculous happenings that she volunteered to witness to them publicly. On numerous occasions and without charge she spoke to rapt audiences in packed lecture halls in the hope that others might share her faith in survival beyond death.

At the time of his ill-fated flight in 1928, Capt. Walter Raymond Hinchliffe was a national hero to the people of Great Britain.

He had been a daring flying ace in the World War, had shot down seven German planes and won the Distinguished Flying Cross. In one of his many "dog fights" with his German aerial adversaries, an enemy bullet had punctured his right eye; the black patch he wore over it further added to his mystique. Typical of his flaming courage he was back flying only weeks after the injury.

A lean, handsome man, there was the charisma of an adventurer about him along with the quiet, self-assured sophistication of a man of the world.

Still in his early thirties, he had 9,000 hours of flying time, probably more than anyone else in Britain. After the war he had been blazing new trails for KLM when that great Dutch airline was just starting. Later, he helped his own country launch and develop its first major airline, Imperial Airways.

Hinchliffe was more than simply a skilled, courageous aviator. He was a talented painter, a born sportsman, an avid reader, a student of scientific developments and world affairs, and spoke four languages - in short, he was a veritable Renaissance man.

Above everything else he was a dedicated husband and devoted family man. He loved his wife, Emilie, a tall, beautiful brunette who had captured his heart from the moment they met. This occurred at the time he was KLM's Chief Pilot and she was Executive Secretary to its General Manager. Their enchanted married love affair had blessed them with two wonderful children - Joan, age four and Pam, just four months old. No matter where his flying assignments took him, whether 500 or 3,000 miles away, he always called or cabled his Emilie to let her know he still adored her and to send love to his two precious little ones.

Next to his wife and family, his second passion was the growth and development of aviation. He saw aviation as the means for bringing the different people from many nationalities into one world of peace.

A year prior, on May 21, 1927 he was thrilled, as was the world, by the audacious, solo, non-stop flight of a young American, Charles A. Lindbergh in a single-engine monoplane "The Spirit of St. Louis" from New York to Paris in just 33 hours - a spectacular first in aviation history.

A few weeks later, Clarence Chamberlin and his financial backer, Charles Levine, flew a single-engine Bellanca "The Columbia" 4,000 miles non-stop from New York to Germany.

Then on June 29, 1927 Commander Richard Evelyn Byrd, already famous for his daring 1926 flight over the North Pole, took off with three other veteran crew members in a multi-engined plane "America" from New York to Paris. Although they successful reached their destination, Paris was so smothered in a fog that they could not land; staying aloft until their fuel was exhausted, they ditched their plane just off the coast of France, wading ashore on July 1st, after 42 hours of skillful, non-stop flying--another historic aviation benchmark.[1]

Hinchliffe longed to be a part of such pioneer adventures. He wanted to use his talent to help extend the horizons of aviation as these men had done. For a long time he had contemplated an east-west crossing of the Atlantic from England to New York. He was undaunted by the fact that two of his friends in 1927 had attempted such a crossing in a Fokker, leaving Salisbury Plain, Great Britain for Montreal, but after crossing Ireland and heading out over the Atlantic, had disappeared. Bucking fierce head winds made an east-west crossing of the Atlantic a lot more formidable than a west-east flight with those winds behind you increasing your speed. An east-west crossing slowed your speed, required much more fuel, a stronger plane and a lot more personal stamina. With his skills and experience, with painstaking planning and the right plane, he was sure he could meet the challenge.

Also, he was aware that his days of flying were inevitably numbered. The vision in his one good eye was decreasing. If he was ever to do anything of the stature of the flights of Lindbergh, Chamberlin and Byrd, it must be now. Not only was fame at stake; such a flight could insure financial security for himself and his family for the rest of their lives.

He talked this over with Emilie. They were at one in his career development; she lived with him in spirit in his flights and took a consuming interest in his future plans. She understood the risks of the venture he dreamed of, but knew that he would do nothing foolhardy.

Hinchliffe assured Emilie that if he undertook such a flight, he would insist that his sponsor take out a £10,000 sterling life insurance policy on her behalf - close to half a million dollars on today's exchange. Thus, even if, God forbid, the flight resulted in his death, he would leave his family financially secure.

Despite his stiff bargaining conditions, much to his amazement, he readily found a backer. Or rather, a backer sought him. Elsie Mackay was the elegant daughter of James Lyle Mackay, better known in the press as Lord Inchape, the international shipping magnate whose luxury liners of the P. & O. Shipping Line profitably plied the Orient.

Elsie Mackay was frequently featured in rotogravure, style and social sections of the British press. At 34, she was a brilliant actress of both the London stage and the British cinema, an accomplished horsewoman, a skilled aviator and one of the richest heiresses of England.

Her latest ambition was to be the first woman to fly the Atlantic.

Even though she had not yet met him, Miss Mackay decided the distinguished Capt. Hinchliffe should be her pilot on this venture. She found out from the British Air Ministry how to get in touch with him, and immediately hired him. At their first meeting she gave him a generous monthly retainer to cover all necessary preparations for an east-west flight from England to New York, gave him carte blanche to pick his own plane for their flight and sent him to the United States to purchase it. She granted him all the prize money and agreed to insure his life for £10,000 sterling.

The plane Hinchliffe purchased while in the United States was a Stinson Detroiter, 32 feet long, with a single-engine 200 horse-power Whirlwind motor and a speed capacity of 128 miles an hour - which seems very slow today, but was impressive in 1928.

Months of concentrated preparation followed with Hinchcliffe supervising every detail of assembly of the new plane at Messers. Vickers Works at the Brooklands aerodrome. He installed a new drift indicator and a specially designed aircraft compass. Having studied the aircraft's cruising speed and petrol consumption, with the help of Air Ministry experts he developed charts and plotted alternative courses. Chemical precautions were taken against the possible formation of ice on wings and fuselage. He procured the Air Ministry's permission to use the longer runway of the RAF aerodrome at Cranwell because of the extra heavy fuel load at the take-off.

Before the flight, Miss Mackay assured both Hinchliffe and Emilie that she had put two checks in the mail, one for the premium for the £10,000 life insurance policy and the second for the captain's six weeks service plus many expenses during all the special preparations.

The morning of take-off finally came - March 13, 1928. After tearful goodbyes, the heavily loaded plane sped down the long runway, slowly lifting into the air at 8:35 A.M.

The last words Hinchliffe entered in the plane's logbook were, "My confidence in the success of our venture is now 100%." Mrs. Hinchliffe in her book *The Return of Captain Hinchliffe* added, "We, who loved him, were equally confident. The remotest possibility of failure occurred to none of us."

There was a report of the plane being spotted over Ireland 5 hours later - at 1:40 P.M. That was the first and only report.

Then silence.

Silence for days - stretching into weeks.

Every day for the first week after take-off the tabloids featured a front-page news-story headlined: "Hinchliffe and Mackay Still Missing." But then, presuming them to be dead, the newspapers and radio turned to other more newsworthy events. The world went on while Emilie was left alone to hope and pray.

A full month passed.

On April 13th, thirty days from the date of their take-off, she received the following letter from a Mrs. Beatrice Earl:

> Dear Mrs. Hinchliffe,
>
> Will you excuse a perfect stranger writing to you. I am supposing you are the wife of Mr. Hinchliffe, the airman, lost the other day. I get writing, and I had a communication from him the other day, that they came down into the sea, off the leeward islands, at night, etc. His great anxiety is to communicate with you. Of course

you may not believe in the possibility of
communication, but he has been urgent, three
times, that I must write to you and risk it.
yours sincerely,
Beatrice Earl

The letter did not thrill her. Almost automatically, she assumed Mrs.
Earl to be a crank. She was further turned off because she had no belief
in life after death. Her faith in traditional religious beliefs was practically
nil. Her children had been baptized as a concession to convention, but
she almost never went to church. While she believed in a higher power
and privately said prayers to that power, her faith was rooted in hope
rather than fervent conviction.

In her book *The Return of Captain Hinchliffe,* she recalled one
Sunday morning when both she and Ray had read an article on the
subject of life after death by Hannen Swaffer in *The Sunday Express* which
cited many notables who had arrived at a firm belief in humankind's
survival beyond the grave because of psychic evidence.

Among the highly respected people mentioned in the article were
Sir Arthur Conan Doyle, Sir Oliver Lodge, the French philosopher Henry
Bergson, the psycho-analyst Carl Jung, and the former prime minister of
England, the Earl of Balfour, who was convinced that years after her
untimely death, mediums had put him in touch with a woman he still
deeply loved. All this was unbelievable to her and to Ray. As she noted
in her book, Ray's comment was a light-hearted but scornful, "Absurd
and impossible!" and she agreed.

Accompanying Mrs. Earl's letter to Emilie were the brief transcripts
of her communication with an entity alleging to be her husband -
transmitted via an ouija board! This further raised her doubts.

Emilie knew about the ouija board as did almost everyone in Britain and the United States at that time; she gave the "toy" little credence. It had become a "craze" in the twenties, a parlor game to lighten dull parties. Its players found that among weird or nonsensical messages, sometimes amazingly accurate answers would be found.

It was a simple device which since ancient times in the China of Confucius (551-479 B.C.) and in the Greece of Pythagoras (about 540 B.C.) had been used as a means of alleged communication with discarnates or one's own subconscious. Today's ouija board consisted of an 18" x 12" (or thereabouts) smooth piece of cardboard or waxed masonite with the alphabet printed around its edges, a "yes" on one side and a "no" on the other. Messages were received through a light pointer on which one rested a finger waiting for some invisible force to glide it to various letters, or answering "yes" or "no" to questions.[2]

Despite Emilie's negative reaction to Mrs. Earl's letter, her life-long skepticism about immortality and her dubious view of the ouija board, nevertheless the transcripts of Mrs. Earl's conversations with her alleged husband gave her pause. She could not help reading them over and over.

The first message received by Mrs. Earl, on March 31st read:

Unidentified entity: *Can you help a man who was drowned?*

Mrs. Earl: Who are you?

Unidentified entity: *I was drowned with Elsie Mckay.*

Mrs. Earl: (linking Miss Mckay with Hinchliffe);

How did it happen?

Hinchliffe: *Fog, storm, winds. Went straight down from great height.*

Mrs. Earl: Where did it happen?

Hinchliffe: *Off leeward islands. Tell my wife I want to speak to her. Am in great distress.*

The second message, dated April 11th read:

Hinchliffe: *Tell my wife I want to speak to her.*

103

Mrs. Earl: Where did you say you went down?

Hinchliffe: *Off leeward islands, straight down. I must speak to my wife.*

Mrs. Earl: Where shall I find her?

Hinchliffe: *Purley, if letter does not reach, apply Drummonds, High Street, Croydon. Please find out what I say is correct.*

Then on April 12th a third pleading message for help, read:

Hinchliffe: *Please let my wife know, Mrs. Earl, I implore you.*

Mrs. Earl: It is such a risk, she won't believe perhaps.

Hinchliffe: *Take the risk, my life was all risks: I must speak to her!*

Despite her initial doubts Emilie was haunted by Mrs. Earl's letter and the three messages from her husband Ray - if it actually was Ray. In particular, the second message surprised her - for her home was in Purley and Drummonds was, indeed, Ray's solicitor and did have his office on High Street in Croydon. She was amazed that such correct information could have come to Mrs. Earl through an ouija board. On the other hand, the reference to "leeward islands" seemed preposterous.

Referring to Mrs. Earl's letter in her book, she said, "Having often read in novels about mediums who were usually frauds whose chief concern was the extracting of money from credulous dupes, I hesitated to reply to it." Again she recalled Ray's comments about the psychic realm: "Absurd and impossible!"

Something, however, prevented her from dropping the subject. Because it wouldn't leave her mind she turned to her friends asking if they knew anything about spiritualism. Like the majority of the human race, they readily responded that they knew nothing about it, then, quite as readily ridiculed the whole idea.

104

Still, despite their negative comments and Ray's blanket dismissal of the whole psychic field, she found it impossible to turn Mrs. Earl's letter off.

A line in the third transcript, *"Take the risk, my whole life was all risks!"* wrenched something inside her and brought tears to her eyes - Ray could have said that.

On April 12th, the same day she wrote to Emilie Hinchliffe, Mrs. Earl also wrote to Sir Arthur Conan Doyle, enclosing a second copy of the transcripts. Fearing she might be deceiving herself she wanted his counsel.

The following day she felt impelled to try the ouija board again. After a brief period of silence, the pointer under her fingers slowly began to move, spelling out:

"Thank you for what you have done. My wife still hopes I am alive. Glad you have told Doyle."

The message made her feel less foolish as it confirmed the validity of the previous communications.

When Sir Arthur got her letter, he immediately checked the phone book for the name and address of Hinchliffe's solicitor. He was much impressed that the discarnate came through with the correct name and address - something Mrs. Earl could not have known.

As a precaution he suggested that Mrs. Earl veryify the import of her messages against the findings of a reliable trance medium in whom he placed great trust, Mrs. Eileen Garrett. He asked permission to make an appointment for a seance with Mrs. Garrett for her.

Mrs. Earl readily assented for she was personally familiar with Mrs. Garrett's splendid work. Some years prior when she had apparently contacted her son through the ouija board after his death in World War

I and feared she might be deluding herself, she had turned to Mrs. Garrett at the London Spiritualist Alliance, and received confirmation.

Just as Mrs. Garrett's findings had substantiated the fact that her son was happy and thriving on the Other Side, her seance with her April 18th completely verified the information she had previously received from Capt. Hinchliffe.

After a few pleasantries had been exchanged, Mrs. Garrett, breathing deeply, quickly sank into a trance and the heavy voice of her control, Uvani, came through.

> Uvani: *Greetings, my friend, I hope I may be of some help.*
>
> Mrs. Earl: Can you tell me anything about Captain Hinchliffe?
>
> Uvani: *Yes. He has been about you a great deal. He thinks he has succeeded well with you.*
>
> Mrs. Earl: Can you tell me what happened?
>
> Uvani: *He went far out of his course. South. Five hundred miles or so south.*
>
> Mrs. Earl: Was the machine injured?
>
> Uvani: *No.*
>
> Mrs. Earl: Was he short of petrol?
>
> Uvani: *Had not enough to land anywhere. Buffeted about by wind, rain and storm.*
>
> Mrs. Earl: Did he suffer?
>
> Uvani: *No. It happened too quickly...His great anxiety is his wife. He wants to speak to her. I don't think his wife is English. There is a small baby, I believe, and I am not sure if there is another child.*

Mrs. Earl was pleased to note that the information received corroborated her earlier messages. What elated her most was that Captain Hinchliffe still lived! That was what was most important.

To date, Mrs. Earl had received no response from the famous aviator's wife to her April 12th letter. With this additional good news to relay to her, she fervently prayed she would hear soon. While awaiting a reply, she posted her long-hand record of the seance to Dr. Conan Doyle.

In May of 1928, although he did not know it, Sir Arthur had less than 26 months to live on earth. His drive and spirit seemed tireless as he continued his exhausting speaking and writing schedule.

Every day he received more than 60 letters from people like Mrs. Earl asking for his help. Despite his busy schedule and demanding public life, he found time to answer them all.

Mrs. Earl's second letter with her long-hand minutes of her seance with Mrs. Garret now fully convinced him that Mrs. Earl was dealing with an authentic, evidential case. He found this particularly poignant because he was familiar with Captain Hinchliffe's daring exploits, had admired him greatly and felt his passing a great loss to aviation. Now he longed to reach out and comfort his widow and to reassure her that her husband still lived. On May 14, 1928 he wrote:

Dear Mrs. Hinchliffe,

May I express my deep sympathy in your grief.

I wonder if you received a letter from a Mrs. Earl. She has had what looks like a true message from your husband, sending his love and assurance that all was well with him. I have every reason to believe Mrs. Earl to be trustworthy and the fact that the message contains the correct address of a solicitor, known to your husband and not to Mrs. Earl is surely notable.

A second medium corroborated the message. The medium remarked that you were not English and had a baby and she

107

thought another child. I should be interested to know if that is correct. If not, it does not affect the message of the first medium. I am writing on what appears to be your husband's request in bringing the matter before you. According to the message, the plane was driven far south. I allude to it in a guarded way in my notes in *The Sunday Express* next week.

Please let me have a line.

yours faithfully,

A. Conan Doyle

When she received his letter, Emilie was surprised and touched that a person of Dr. Conan Doyle's world-wide fame would take the trouble to write to her - and to write with such care and concern.

Saturday afternoon, May 19th, 1928, Emilie met with Mrs. Earl at Mrs. Earl's home. She found her hostess to be kindness itself, an open-hearted woman whose only motive seemed to be that she wanted to help others as she had been helped following the loss of her son in the Great War.

Mrs. Earl spoke movingly of how she had been sustained during that difficult time. Messages from her son on the ouija board and the corroboration she had subsequently received through the seances with Mrs. Garrett made her positive that her son lived in the next dimension.

The two women had a fascinating two hour discussion over tea. Emilie listened entranced, forgetting for the moment her natural skepticism over things occult.

As a next step Mrs. Earl suggested that even though she felt the messages she had received via the ouija board were authentic, it might be better if Emilie tried a trance medium such as Mrs. Garrett. She pointed out that an ouija board might prove a bit slow for Captain Hinchliffe whom she sensed had a great many things he urgently wanted to say to his wife. Grateful for her suggestion, Emilie asked Mrs. Earl to set up an appointment with Mrs. Garrett as soon as possible.

Returning home that afternoon, despite the obvious sincerity of Mrs. Earl, Emilie was still in a quandary about what to think of the psychic realm. Once again, she was overwhelmed by doubts.

She longed to believe that her beloved Ray still lived, even if on some vaguely described "different plane" or invisible "other dimension." Just to know that he still lived would have meant more to her than anything in the world. But could she dare to believe?

"I don't believe anything," she confessed to her friends that evening, having related to them the whole story of her meeting with Mrs. Earl. She was totally perplexed. "It may or may not be true."

Then her eyes lost their softness and her lips tightened into a straight, hard line. "It may or may not be true, but I'm going to find out!" she vowed determinedly.

From the start she had grave foreboding about going to a seance and had frankly confessed to Mrs. Earl that she would be grateful if her friend would accompany her. The thought of an hour cooped up in a strange, dark room with a total stranger who was lost in an unconscious trance and talking in someone else's voice gave her "the creeps."

Mrs. Earl escorted her to the white-columned town-house of the London Spiritualist Alliance. On the second floor off a commodious library of psychic books, she and Mrs. Earl were ushered into a gracefully furnished sitting room with a cheerful blaze in the fireplace and sunlight streaming through the windows. The bright sunlight particularly reassured

Emilie since she was determined to keep a stenographic record of the seance and in the clear daylight she could easily take down in shorthand everything that was said.

Her surprise continued when she met Eileen Garrett. Here was no witchlike gypsy psychic with her hand out for a fee, but instead, an elegantly dressed, attractive woman whose soft, radiant face, beautiful blue-green eyes, generous mouth and infectious, winning smile instantly signaled her warm personal magnetism.

To her further surprise, Mrs. Earl purposely introduced her to Mrs. Garrett without giving her name - simply as a friend who was accompanying her. As it turned out, despite Mrs. Earl's precaution, the seance immediately revealed the personality of her husband.

Emilie was forewarned by both Mrs. Earl and Mrs. Garrett that when Eileen Garrett went into a trance, a guide or "control," presumably from the Other Side, would temporarily take over the body of the sleeping medium through her vocal organs. Nevertheless, she was taken aback to find that after Mrs. Garrett had stretched, yawned, moaned slightly and then completely passed out in a trance state of seeming unconsciousness, her guide began speaking through her in a low male voice with a marked foreign accent, introducing himself as Uvani.

What surprised and amazed Emilie most of all was that the entity alleging to be her husband came through with 25 pieces of astonishingly accurate information, some of these items so personal no one but her own dear Ray could possibly have known them.

Here is the essence of the seance's dialogue as Emilie heard it and transcribed it - with her comments, which were made at a later time:

Uvani: *You are a newcomer, you have not been here before. There are two or three people round you. There is firstly a lady, aged about 62-65, a small figure, name is Elise Elizabeth.*

Emilie: I recognized her as my grandmother who passed away in 1901.

Uvani: *Here comes some one dear to you, a very young man. He went out suddenly. He was very vivacious and full of life. He passed due to strong congestion of the heart and lungs but was in a state of unconsciousness.*

Emilie: Due to drowning.

Uvani: *He shows me portraits, he mentions the name Joan - little Joan.*

Emilie: My husband always called his elder daughter 'Little Joan.'

Uvani: *He was full of strength, he was full of speed, perhaps cars or planes. He passed after having flown in an aeroplane. He was 33.*

Emilie: All four points correct.

Uvani: *He suffers with the eyes, he keeps rubbing over one eye and is laughing. What has happened to one eye?*

Emilie: He used to wear an eyeshade as a result of a war wound.

Uvani: *He must be your husband, he keeps pointing to a ring on a finger.*

Emilie: Correct.

Uvani: *He talks of a little baby, the baby is not alone. He is referring to a little girl again, whom he calls Joan.*

Uvani: *In his possession he had a portrait of Joan when he passed over.*

Emilie: Correct again.

Uvani: *He asks: Have you the watch he gave you with his name on it?*

Emilie: A watch my husband gave me three months before his passing.

Uvani: *He says: Don't worry about his watch, he had it with him, the one with the inscription on it, which was given him as a presentation.*

Emilie: I had wondered where this watch of my husband's was, as two days before he left, I had noticed

111

the strap was broken, and I was puzzled as to whether he had taken it with him. I had not mentioned it to anyone.

Uvani: *Have you got the bangle with you, he gave you?*

Emilie: I was wearing it. It was an engagement gift.

Uvani: *Your husband mentions several names of people he has seen; there is for instance Herman and Wilhelm. He has seen them both here.*

Emilie: Recognized. Both flyer friends of my husband. Herman, a pilot killed in Holland in 1925, Wilhelm killed in a flying accident in 1926.

A short description of Hinchliffe's last flight followed. Emilie transcribed it exactly as it was given. She was moved by the fact that though the voice was that of Uvani, "the words were those of my husband."

Uvani: (Hinchliffe now speaking directly through him) *I left in the morning and was in the plane one day and one night. At two o'clock was the last sight of land.*

Emilie: Correct.

Uvani: *Then eight hours of steady flying, the currents were strong, visibility was bad, sea calm, fog, and it was later on, about 400 miles out, that I met storms.*

Emilie: Correct again. Confirmed by government weather chart for the day of flight.

Uvani: *I flew west-north-west course, and my main intention was to keep north, to keep on a northerly course.*

Emilie: It was always his intention to keep north.

Uvani: *I had hoped to go on to Labrador, this was my intention in case of trouble. However, the more I flew north, the more I was buffeted about and it was impossible to live in it. I flew in a west-north-*

west direction at the rate of 80-90 miles per hour, from 2 p.m. until 10 p.m. so that I had flown practically 700 miles. At 10 p.m. I altered my course to a little more north and I flew in this direction for another two hours until midnight, so that I covered therefore another 200 miles (or nearly).

At midnight the gale became terrible, I got into sleet and rain also. The gale broke one strut of the machine and another strut cracked, and I realized it would be impossible to reach America, and I then thought of the leeward islands.

Emilie: The islands to the leeward, meaning the Azores. This explains Mrs. Earl's receiving the communication, mentioned earlier, concerning the leeward islands.

Uvani: (his tone now like an excited witness at a disaster) *At midnight I therefore deliberately changed my course to due south. I did so in order to attempt to reach these islands. You will find this difficult to believe, as I had always told you that I would go north in case of trouble, but did change my course to due south. From midnight until 3 a.m. I flew on this southerly course. I cannot be sure of my course, I only know south, because my compass had gone wrong. I went south to get out of the gale. A plug in the engine oiled up and the canvas was tearing.*

The aeroplane could not live in the gale and I was buffeted about terribly. I was clean taken off of my course and often did not know myself on what course I was.

At 1 a.m. I abandoned hope. Terror never! But the anguish, knowing every half-hour might be the end!

I remembered the correct course exactly, but I had to change course. I went south to get out of the gale and in the hope of reaching the islands.

After 3 a.m. hovered near water and machine became water logged. I was then within sight of the Azores, I could only see some rocks, but it was impossible to reach them owing to the currents...I was drowned twenty minutes after leaving the wreck. I became unconscious and came into death quick.

Emilie: I have since received the actual position at which my husband states he struck the water. Latitude and longitude were given and the position shown on a small chart, illustrating the Azores.

Uvani: (bringing up a random bit of conclusive evidence from Hinchliffe) *He gave his mother a shock once when he fell in a tree.*

Emilie: Correct. When shot down in France, my husband's machine fell in a tree.

Uvani: (speaking again directly as Capt. Hinchliffe) *You have been worried about finances. You have been waiting, waiting, waiting. But you will hear good news soon.*

Emilie: His mention of financial concern was correct!

Uvani: *Your husband says that you knew he wanted to do it. He was coming to the end of his flying, he could not have flown very much longer, his eyes were not as good as they used to be and he wanted to give it up, although flying was his life. He often talked with you about his enterprise and he did it to provide for you.*

Emilie: Again correct.

Uvani: *I cannot say his name but see signatures all round. I will spell it: EFFILHCNIH, I see in a glass.*

Emilie: Backwards but accurate.

Uvani: (in a voice of great anguish reflecting Hinchliffe's feelings) *Oh, God! Oh, God! It was awful! From one until three o'clock! He had forgotten everything but his wife and children! As he grows stronger, he will communicate better. His last superhuman effort was to try to swim to land.* (after a long pause, as though speaking directly for the airman) *Tell them there is no death but everlasting*

114

life. Life here is but a journey and a change to different conditions. We go on from unconscious perfection to conscious perfection.

All the above is a matter of record in Emilie's book, *The Return of Capt. Hinchliffe.*

As she folded up her stenographic pad and put away her pencil, Emilie sank back into her chair, physically and emotionally drained yet at the same time highly exhilarated.

Viewed objectively, the seance had to be judged as one of the most extraordinary evidential sessions in the annals of psychic history. Increasing its validity was the fact that it was witnessed by another person - namely Mrs. Earl, and was exactly transcribed word-for-word in Emilie's expert stenography.

For Emilie, despite her prior determination to be hard-headed and skeptical, the seance was anything *but* objective! All the many reminders of her darling, dashing Ray and their beautiful love together and his adoration for their children brought an ache to her throat and filled her heart with longing for her perfect mate.

As her beloved related the story of his last three hours on earth when he knew he was doomed, she shared his hopeless, anguished tension. When he spoke of the last 20 minutes in the water after the plane had crashed, tears streamed down her cheeks as she went through the agony of his death as though with him.

On the other hand, what exhilarated her and gave her new hope was the fact that someone - it almost *had* to be her husband - had somehow managed to tell her so many revealing and telling details about their life together, their children and other personal matters, matters so personal that only Ray could have known them. In view of this, then it logically followed, that somehow - somewhere - Ray must still be alive.

115

To claim that Mrs. Garrett or Uvani had read her mind and this was simply a demonstration of telepathy could not possibly explain the vivid description of Ray's ill-fated flight with all the technical details which only a flyer could have known.

She found her skepticism floundering in the face of such evidence. It was all so overwhelming. She closed her eyes and prayed inwardly to that Higher Power she had always hoped existed. "Oh, dear God, if only it could be true. If only Ray *really - truly - actually* still lived!"

"Eileen Garrett talked with the dead, healed the sick, predicted the future. She performed miracles for fifty years with undiminished and frightening accuracy. She made no claims to having supernatural powers, and said she was not a miracle worker but merely had a sensitivity, highly developed perhaps, which enabled her to see and do things impossible for most people. She also said that most people could, with training, become equally sensitive...And yet Eileen Garrett's psychic feats always overwhelmed those who worked with her on any enterprise." Thus wrote Allan Angoff, who served Mrs. Garrett for 25 years as an editor, writer, creative programmer and warm friend, in his biography of her, *Eileen Garrett and the World Beyond the Senses* (1974)[3]

Unfortunately most of those today who profess to have psychic talents for sale to the public are not only untrained but are often no more gifted psychically than the rest of us. The amount of fraud in the psychic field has always been and still is horrendous.

Mrs. Gladys Osborne Leonard was similarly mystified by her own brilliant talents and submitted to endless research tests by scientists of the British Society for Psychical Research. Also, Mrs. Leonora Piper's awe-inspiring psychic feats were examined and probed for years by Professor

116

William James of Harvard University and other investigators of the American and British Societies for Psychical Research.

In similar fashion Eileen Garrett freely submitted to investigations by distinguished researchers: Dr. William Brown of the Parapsychology Laboratory of Oxford University; Dr. Anita Muhl, physician and psychiatrist with the Special Education Division of the State of California; Dr. Adolf Meyer of the Psychiatric Clinic of Johns Hopkins University; the renowned French physician, Dr. Alexis Carrel, of the Rockefeller Institute, winner of the Nobel Prize in Medicine; Dr. Gardner Murphy of Columbia University, who later became Director of Research for the Menninger Clinic in Topeka, Kansas; the psychologist, Dr. William McDougall of Duke University; and Dr. J. B. Rhine, who founded Duke University's Parapsychology Laboratory and proved scientifically the reality of extra-sensory perception.

In 1951, a decade after she had come to the U.S., became an American citizen and formed a successful publishing house, Creative Age Press, she founded the Parapsychology Foundation to further psychic research through conferences, publications and financial grants for special projects. Every year since 1953, the Foundation has convened an international conference of outstanding scholars dealing with some important aspect of psychic phenomena. Since Mrs. Garrett's death in 1970 these conferences have continued under the leadership of her daughter, Mrs, Eileen Colby. The Eileen J. Garrett Library is open to the public in New York City.

A prolific writer in her later years, Mrs. Garrett authored several books on parapsychology, four novels and three biographies: *My Life in Search of the Meaning of Mediumship, Adventures in the Supernormal, and Many Voices.*

117

One of the most dramatic and impressive seances of Eileen Garrett's career occurred October 7th, 1930, two days after the crash and explosion of the British dirigible R101 in France in which all of its passengers, officers and staff, with the exception of four badly injured crewmen, were destroyed.

This remarkable seance occurred at the National Laboratory of Psychical Research in London in the presence of its director, the well known ghost hunter Harry Price, and Australian newspaperman, Ian Coster. Also present was Price's secretary, Ethel Beenham, who took word-for-word notes. The Commander of the R101, Flight Lieutenant H. C. Irwin, who had been killed in the crash, suddenly appeared in Mrs. Garrett's trance and cried out in an anguished voice: *"The whole bulk of the dirigible was...too much for her engine capacity... Useful lift too small. Gross lift computed badly... Elevator jammed. Oil pipe plugged..."*

As Allan Angoff described the seance, "On and on went the voice of the dead Irwin, with quantities of technical details, all of which were noted verbatim by Miss Beenham... Experts at the Royal Airship Works in Bedford, who later read the notes, called it 'an astounding document,' replete with confidential details."[4]

Months after the crash many of the observations in Mrs. Garrett's message from Flight Lieutenant Irwin tallied in detail with the findings of the official British Air Ministry inquiry.

This brief acquaintance with Eileen Garrett will enable you to more fully appreciate the significance of her psychic gifts and revelations to Mrs. Hinchliffe as we continue Captain Hinchliffe's story as told by him from the Other Side.

Immediately after the seance with Mrs. Garrett, at the suggestion of Mrs. Earl, Emilie phoned Dr. Conan Doyle as a courtesy to let him know what happened. Sir Arthur was not only delighted to receive her call but wanted to personally hear her full story and invited both women to come at once to his home for tea.

When they arrived, he welcomed them warmly and listened avidly as Emilie breathlessly recounted her incredible experience at the seance. Her voice was filled with wonder and excitement at its amazingly accurate revelations yet also expressed her lingering doubts about the whole episode.

"To believe in the impossible takes time and study," Sir Arthur responded with a smile, noting it had taken him a full 34 years.

He urged her to continue her seances with Mrs. Garrett and to further explore the psychic field. Quietly and movingly, he related how he and his wife Jean had found solace after the passing of her brother Malcolm, his brother Innes and his oldest son Kingsley, thanks to the irrefutable evidence through seances that their loved ones lived on. He fervently hoped that she would find the same comfort in the sure knowledge that there was no death - "just as your husband promised at the end of the your seance today."

For Emilie the meeting with Sir Arthur was reassuring and inspiring. Sir Arthur was even more impressive than she had expected - a warm human being whose sensitivity and thoughtfulness were larger than life.

Returning home by taxi in the grey cold of oncoming evening her mood abruptly changed as she thought about her financial situation. In vain she checked her mailbox for a letter from Lord Inchcape, Elsie Mackay's father. It had been six weeks since she had asked her husband's law firm to look into the £10,000 insurance policy Elsie Mackay had promised her husband as part of their flight agreement. Although just before take-off Elsie had assured both of them she had just put the premium check in the mail to her insurance carrier, her husband's lawyers after a careful investigation had discovered that *no* policy had ever been taken out.

119

It seems that Miss Mackay in good faith had indeed written and mailed a £2,600 premium check for the £10,000 policy to her insurance company just prior to the flight, but there were insufficient funds in her bank account to cover the check. Consequently, the insurance company did not write up the policy and denied any obligation for coverage.

Miss Mackay did have sufficient money in other accounts. There was no question about the size of her wealth. Her net worth ranked her among England's richest.

With Miss Mackay's presumed death, her assets were immediately frozen and her father, as designated executor of her will, became the temporary custodian of everything she owned. In view of the fact that he had adamantly forbade his daughter to join Capt. Hinchliffe on the flight, an order she had secretly but whole-heartedly disobeyed, Emilie was not at all sure what he might now do. Still she could not help but believe he would feel impelled to honor his daughter's obligations, particularly since the £10,000 of promised coverage would mean life-long security for her and her two children and was nothing to a tycoon of Lord Inchcape's immense wealth and his daughter's estate was also gigantic.

As her only recourse, Emily had written to Lord Inchcape in the prayerful hope that he would honor his daughter's promise. That was over six weeks ago!

During the ensuing weeks, she had twice more written pleading for his help. To date there was no reply although it was obvious her letters had been delivered for they had not been returned. It would seem that her petitions were deliberately being ignored.

For two months she had been living on savings that were fast depleting. She needed money, need it desperately and needed it now. She thought of Ray's remark about finances in the seance only that afternoon: *"You have been worried about finances. You have been waiting, waiting, waiting. But you will hear good news soon."*

If indeed that had really been Ray speaking - did Ray really know? And how long was *soon?* Another week? Another month? Or two or three months? She wondered how long her financial resources could last?

Later that evening, her children asleep, as she began transcribing Mrs. Garrett's words from stenography into legible, typed text she found herself yearning for Ray's possible help. If any of what went on that day in the seance was at all true, perhaps he could somehow intervene, reach Lord Inchcape and move him to honor Elsie's commitment.

Then she abruptly stopped herself. That kind of thinking was neither rational nor logical - it was downright ridiculous. Ray's earlier comment about psychic phenomena came back to her: "Absurd and impossible."

Still, despite her doubts, despite her skeptical reservations, as she continued her transcriptions one thing seemed to become clear to her: as Sir Arthur had urged she *knew* she must go on with the seances.

In her second seance with Mrs. Garrett on May 24th, the evidence became even more specific. Despite her doubts, Emilie found herself deeply moved by the warm and intimate import of the messages.

Opening the session, Uvani embarked at once on a most accurate description of her beloved Ray:

There is a gentleman who seems very close to you. He is in great trouble. He is young, bright. He has a delightful personality, and gives me an impression of strength in a protective way, and gives me the feeling of great cheerfulness. He has been getting in touch with you. He is very tall, slight and I think has light brown hair, blue eyes, straight nose. He is a rather strong man. He has been in the Army, held a commission in the Army. I think he still holds it... He was killed very quickly. He wants to speak to you privately. He says he is your husband.

121

Then, the man who claimed to be her husband, through Uvani, described their home in a most personal way, as though he had lived there for years:

He remembers the dining room, the garden and the garage on the side of the house, and the house next door. He used to whistle from the garage to you in the bedroom. The bedroom looks out on the garden. He mentions the bookcase, the little occasional table, his portraits in flying clothes and the one in Army uniform. There is also the wireless and he often sees you sitting by the wireless. There are many things which he brought you from different places. In the hall, his cap and coats are still there. You have left them as they were. He used to work in the garden on Sundays and with Joan, talking to Joan in the garden while she helped him. He is devoted to her. He refers to the dog. He is fond of him. He often sees him running around the house...

Every detail was correctly pictured and poignantly accurate. Then, much to her amazement, Ray brought up his small daughter's inquiry about him only that morning:

He knows you have told Joan that he has gone on a journey and that she asked when he was coming back. He does thank you for keeping it from her. Give a kiss to Joan and the baby.

Both she and Ray were talented amateur painters and he mentioned the oil paintings of the children on which she had been working to pass the long, desolate days since his final flight:

He has seen the portraits you have painted of Joan and the baby since he has left.

He spoke of their children's governess by name and commented on her fine care of their children:

Betty is careful. She is trustworthy and is careful with both children.

Somehow he seemed to know she had been looking for his studs - a small detail, but how could anyone but Ray possibly know this? Regarding this, Uvani said:

He knows you sorted out the papers in his desk and drawers. The studs are in a little box in the cupboard. He saw you tidy his papers.

In her book Emilie wrote: "He knew I had been wondering where his studs were and he described exactly where I should find them. Subsequent investigation revealed the studs exactly as described."

More evidence continued to come through. Ray, through Uvani, referred to at least a dozen people whom he had known and whom he had met again on the Other Side. He mentioned when they passed over and in some cases where and how.

Ray briefly re-described his ordeal over the ocean and his battle with the gale and storm, then followed this with the specific name of the island in the Azores near which he had to abandon his plane:

The name of the island is Maro - Cauro - or Caro - no, Carvo.

Immediately after the seance, Emilie checked this out on one of Ray's Air Ministry maps, enlisting the help of his trusted right-hand man Gordon Sinclair. Together they found the exact island Ray had mentioned - of which neither she nor Gordon had known. It wasn't Carvo - Uvani had mispronounced it - it was *Corvo* and Ray now obviously knew precisely the island near which he had landed.

He spoke specifically of the engine trouble he had endured and especially of his problem with his airplane's spark plugs. He mentioned he had had them changed just before his last flight, something no one could have known except for Ray and his assistant Sinclair. As Uvani put it, speaking for Ray:

He was never sure about his plugs. And in the end, before he started, he changed the plugs... He was nervous about the plugs, and he wanted to change the make of the plugs. He was a little shaky over the plugs

123

because he had not tried these on a long distance flight. He said one was not sparking and that cost him; because there is no hope as soon as anything like this begins. There was much backfiring...

Emilie checked this point with Gordon immediately following the seance. Gordon affirmed that he and Ray had, indeed, changed the spark plugs just before the flight!

Once again he sought to reassure her regarding her financial crisis: *He wants you to remember that the financial matters will be all right. Carry on with the house and the car. He knows you will get the money.*

When the seance ended, the sum total of the evidence seemed to Emilie quite overwhelming. It had greatly strengthened her growing conviction that she was *truly* speaking to her beloved husband.

Only a few days later the evidence mounted when Mrs. Earl sitting alone, felt moved to tune in on her ouija board. Three statements were especially personal and telling:

1. *"Hinchliffe."* (identifying himself) *"In the end there will be some kind of settlement."*
2. *"Had small scar on throat. Suffered from throat."* Emilie was impressed by Ray's ingenious efforts to authenticate his identity. In her book she wrote: "In 1923 my husband, owing to the constant irritation felt in his throat, decided to have his tonsils removed. I was probably the only person aware of this operation."
3. *"There is a joke about a molar and a ring, ask my wife."*

When Mrs. Earl queried about this strange message, Emilie's eyes filled up yet she could not help but smile. She explained, "When my husband was a medical student he once had to make as a training

124

exercise, a gold crown for a tooth. When it had finished its sphere of usefulness, he made the same gold into a ring which he wore for years."

It was at this point that Emilie concluded, "For me, at any rate, the numerous little, private trivialities (so-called) which had been a feature of all my husband's communications were largely instrumental in convincing me as to the identity of the intelligence responsible for those communications."

By her third seance on June 9, 1928 Emilie had become fully convinced that she was actually in touch with her husband. As she wrote in the book, "By now skepticism had long since given place to conviction. Once again the scoffer had remained to pray."

It was during this June 9th seance that Ray, through Uvani, quite specifically advised Emilie to got to the press with her financial problems:

His great responsibility is in connection with monetary things. He is desirous and anxious to bring things to a head. He promises you that from the father of the girl there should be some recompensation forthcoming. It seems your husband is worried over Inchcape's attitude. If he will not listen, here is the way out of it. Talk this over with The Daily Express. They will understand what I mean. The name is Lord Beaverbrook. Please do not worry, even though the monetary conditions are low. You are going to get some money so that you can maintain the house and make it possible to carry on. I have the impression that you are getting the money in July. Perfectly certain.

His idea of going to the press at first appalled her. It seemed to her an end to any privacy. Still she promised Ray inwardly she would do as directed as soon as the opportunity presented itself.

Uvani closed the session with Ray's heart-warming assurance:

He will keep near you until you are free of worry. God bless you and your household. Remember there is no death, but everlasting life.

125

She now fully accepted in her heart, mind and soul what Ray had just said: *"there is no death but everlasting life.!"*

Continuing to express his concern about her financial dilemma, at a subsequent seance through Uvani, Ray suggested that she see their solicitors about selling a piece of real estate they had bought some years ago in the hope of one day building on it. After the seance, she looked all over the house to no avail for the blueprint which defined the property. A few days later, while she was visiting Mrs. Earl, Ray made his presence felt, moved Mrs. Earl to get out her ouija board and sent Emilie this message:

You will find the paper which may be of use to house agents
behind a drawer on the left of my desk.

She found the blueprint shoved back behind a left-hand drawer for safekeeping, just as Ray had said.

From that day forward she felt her husband's strength beside her, always there. She knew he would ever be anxious to keep her confident and assist her in resolving financial problems.

In the first week of July Winston Churchill, then Chancellor of the Exchequer, announced in Parliament that Lord Inchcape had decided to give his daughter's entire estate - a fortune of £527,000 sterling, or over $2.5 million dollars, to His Majesty's government to alleviate the National Debt - but not, however until some 50 years hence.

Emilie was aghast at this bizarre announcement. It seemed to her a hollow, grandiose gesture helping no one for half a century and then scarcely touching the real problems of the people of Great Britain. Emilie was further appalled that the weird agreement in no way acknowledged the courageous spirit of Lord Inchcape's audacious daughter. But worse from Emilie's standpoint, it ignored the legitimate debt the Elsie Mackay estate owed to her husband and his family.

Now she saw the wisdom of Ray's entreaty to go to the press. Going to the press was the only recourse she now had left.

Surprisingly, she didn't have to go to the press - the press came to her. Within minutes after the Churchill announcement, a reporter from *The Daily Express* knocked on her door wanting to know how she felt about Lord Inchcape's decision to give his daughter's fortune to the British government.

Emilie gave him the story without rancor, stating the facts of her case. She had written Lord Inchcape several letters from which she had received no response. In them she had asked that he honor the terms of his daughters's agreement with her husband - the promised £10,000 sterling insurance coverage and payment for Ray's last six weeks of service conducted prior to his death.

The subsequent front-page news stories in the nation-wide newspaper syndicates of Lord Beaverbrook and Lord Northcliffe across Britain spelled out her dilemma in heart-breaking headlines such as: "MRS. HINCHLIFFE NEARLY PENNILESS," "BEQUEST OF ELSIE MACKAY IGNORES WIDOW'S CLAIM."

As a consequence of the press outcry, the House of Commons became vocally concerned and Hore Belisha, head of the Liberal Party, publicly questioned why Mrs. Hinchliffe's lawful claim had been ignored by Lord Inchcape. His Lordship's response from his castle in Ayrshire, given through one of his protecting entourage, was a cold, "No Comment."

After a week-long flurry in the media her case seemed to have been dropped and forgotten.

127

While Emilie applied for jobs as a translator and executive secretary, only Ray kept her hopes up with his supporting love and confidence in an ultimate Inchcape settlement. Through Uvani he assured her: *If anything unexpected happens or you get into any dilemma, come to me and let me talk to you. I will help until everything will be cleared up.* (regarding the settlement) *It may run to the last day in July, but it will be in July.*

Despite his prediction, Emilie found herself worried and depressed for the next two weeks. Then unexpectedly, on July 31st, Winston Churchill again appeared before the House of Commons to make this announcement:

> Lord Inchcape being desirous that the Elsie Mackay Fund of £500,000, given by him and Lady Inchcape and their family to the nation, should not be the occasion or object of any complaint by other sufferers from the disaster in which his daughter lost her life, has placed at the disposal of the Chancellor of the Exchequer a further sum of £10,000 sterling from his own property to be applied for the purpose of meeting any complaint in such manner as the Chancellor of the Exchequer in his absolute discretion may think fit.

Though Emilie was not named, the grant was obviously intended for her and her children!

Now the slightest doubt that Emilie had ever had about the authenticity of Ray's existence was washed away. His advice about going to the press had been exactly right, his statements about everything else had been precise and accurate, and now - just as he had predicted - the news of a settlement came on July 31st! This, for Emilie, was the ultimate proof.

128

Having received her settlement some weeks later, now Emilie was determined to pass on to others the simple but astounding message that Ray had twice repeated in seances with Mrs. Garrett - *"there is no death, but eternal life"* - and to offer as proof her own incredible experience. If she, a skeptic, an agnostic, could be convinced there was life after death, then she owed it to give others this message of hope.

She scheduled a public lecture through the Stead Lecture Bureau and enthralled a house of over 400 people (with hundreds turned away), telling her story simply but movingly. She refused any recompense for her speaking. Subsequently she went on spellbinding thousands more with lectures in London and adjacent areas.

To better answer questions concerning the quality of life in the next dimension, Emilie scheduled several more seances with Eileen Garrett. Her husband's sharp intelligence and sensitive insights gave a number of insights corroborating the testimony of Raymond Lodge, Sir Arthur Conan Doyle and Albert Payson Terhune. In his inimitable and illuminating way Capt. Hinchliffe gives us his descriptions of the characteristics of life on the Other Side.

1. He found the transition from the physical body to the ethereal body so painless he scarcely knew he was passing:
Transition from the physical body to the ethereal body occupies only a matter of moments. There is no pain in the severance of the two, and so alike are they, that it is some while - probably in some cases, days - before this transition is noticed. In my case, it was noticed quickly, because I had been conscious of facing death for many hours before actually passing.

2. He found himself quite unchanged yet more awake, more alert, "with a freer mind, housed in a much finer body:"

Actually, I feel no different. Nothing angelic, nothing ethereal, nothing one would think of as being connected with heaven or the hereafter.

My actual experience is that I am as real in this life as I have been to you, and that all growth towards that great happiness and the great heaven they talk of, must be a slower process than most people believe...

Going from one state of life to another, one finds as much difference existing as one would find if, while on earth, one crossed from one side of the world to the other. For each state here has a different standard of thought, as each country in your sphere has a different standard of speech...

I cannot understand why humans say that after death all is happiness, all joy, all rest, all cheerfulness, all brightness. Surely they should be brought to the realization that as they have lived on earth, and worked, and done the right thing, so shall their reward be in the hereafter. Likewise, the man or woman who has taken things easily and at other people's expense while still in the flesh, pays for it on this Side. For though here physical suffering is not, mental suffering is much more severe than it can ever be on earth.

People will say: Why? Because here you are more awake, more alert, more able to perceive things by virtue of possessing a much freer mind housed in a much finer body, which does not blind you so much as did the physical state.

3. He found everyone had a chance to work out his or her salvation, but it was up to each person as an individual. The concepts of heaven and hell are real but the heaven or hell was within each person's soul:

I have not found any evil here. I have found many people, I assure you, who are ignorant of every law, but that does not constitute evil. I find that 'ignorance' is something that is within us from the very beginning, and is as necessary in our make-up as is our strength. For you can learn more by the mistakes you make than by the things you do rightly and well...

There are hells and there are heavens even as we have been taught to believe...There are weak people, dissolute people, vicious people, all seeking to still take part in the life they knew, rather than enter fully into the new life...

There are laboratories full of youth, full of life, all working for good, just as there are others whose energies are mistaken ones. The good are working for the ultimate upliftment of mankind, and the others are not doing much other than trying to keep a state of things on earth as they themselves liked, enjoyed, and knew...

Really there are no evil spirits. There are ignorant ones, interfering ones, malicious ones and blind ones - that is, blind to their own faults - and these constitute the so-called evil here, just as they are the pests of your life...

Each one of the higher states has to be reached by a man's own endeavour, not through the prayers of his friends, though all prayer helps and everything that is asked, if asked for sincerely, is answered somewhere...

Each one of us has an absolutely straight chance of working out his own salvation, irrespective of what he has done

131

or what he may be. This, to me, seems just, and I confess I like it.

4. He found great purpose in the life beyond and he rejoiced in the new knowledge that "your day of usefulness is only dawning when you come over here:"

What do we do? We do everything for which we are fitted. There are huge systems of education, huge laboratories and institutions, that deal with all the conditions for which a man has fitted himself while on earth. Here our necessities are met by mental thought, and are organized and focused... In this state, the mind capacity is larger, more sensitive, and the power of thought intensified...

The organized thought starts here, travels around the spiritual states, gathering strength as it does, and eventually finds its final capacity for work through its human receiver.

None of this destroys free will. Rather, it helps you who are still on the earth I have so lately left, to realize your affinity with those who have gone on, to realize their very great humanity and interest in you. Instead of taking anything away from the beauty of the picture, does it not add to it that your day of usefulness is only dawning when you come over here?

5. He reveled in his work because his energies were free of illness and pain, and the goal of his soul was "to understand and to realize the greatness of the universe:"

I work all the time mentally and in a sense physically, in the things that interest me. One does work. I revel in it, because here in this state, I find myself free, alert and decisive, my energies no longer curtailed or held down by all the pains, ills

132

and depressions, from which the human body can never escape. All these the human body piles up, has had built up for it - an accumulation as it were of all the ills of our parents, grand-parents, and so on - very like rheumatism handed on by the father to the son. But you are free of this accumulation once you have passed on. You have left the lowest plane when you leave the earth because it is then that the soul for the first time becomes conscious of its life, its power of separate existence; though it has existed before, of that I am certain.

What do we work at? We work mentally, and rejoice in so doing, at all the things that kept us busy while on earth - money making excepted...

What is it that makes us wish to work? What makes you work on earth? Ambition! Ambition to have, ambition to be, ambition to possess, and the body overshadows that ambition and teaches the soul that it must have its sustenance - first, last, and always. A very good reason for working, too! But when that struggle is over and there is no longer need to strive after material achievement, the ambition to get and to receive, to make and to possess, does not die with the casting off of the physical make-up. It grows even stronger, only now one desires to possess the gifts for the soul, and the gift of knowledge, and the gift to enable one to see more clearly and to understand and to realize the greatness of the universe in which one now finds himself. For this universe is bigger than anyone realizes... To me it seems immense. To others who have greater knowledge than I, it must be even more stupendous...

I have been here one year but can see everything that happened to me. There are hundreds of people who want to know the reality of what happens when and after passing over.

133

> *These are not thoughts from other people. They are my own.*[5]

The story of Captain Hinchliffe's life beyond this life, thanks to the supernormal psychic genius of Eileen Garrett and the meticulous stenographic transcription skills of his wife, Emilie, is one of the most thoroughly documented and evidential cases in the archives of psychic phenomena.

The Near-Death Experience of a Multitude
of People Who at the Brink of Death Were
Seemingly Granted a Brief Vision of Our
Life to Come - Carefully Documented by
Medical Doctors and Parapsychologists -
Corroborates Other Psychic Evidence of
Life after Death.

There are thousands of people enjoying life today who were at one time pronounced clinically dead.

Somehow, they miraculously survived.

Some have told fantastic and inspiring stories of their brief glimpses of life beyond their so-called "death."

You are presumed to be clinically dead when your heart stops beating, your lungs cease breathing and your brain no longer registers electrical activity on an electroencephalograph.

We have innumerable documented medical cases of hospital patients declared "clinically dead" by attending physicians or nurses who returned to life and related their amazing experiences during the seconds or minutes of apparent physical death.

The person whose best-selling book *Life After Life* first focused public attention in 1975 on the near-death experience and what it is telling us is a medical doctor and psychiatrist - Dr. Raymond A. Moody, Jr.

In his simple yet profoundly stirring book, Dr. Moody recorded and compared the experiences of 150 persons who died, or almost died, and then recovered. He included interviews with 50 of these people who had undergone such a "round-trip" experience. While his was not the first to study such visions, it was the first to bring the near-death experience into nationwide consciousness.

The well known phrase "near death experience" which often becomes NDE in shorthand - is one Dr. Moody coined as the most apt to describe what had previously been referred to as "otherworld journeys" or "near-visions."

Exactly what is the near-death experience? The 150 cases which Moody studied in his classic book of only 184 pages show many striking similarities.

In a number of cases, the patients felt themselves leaving their physical bodies, sometimes only moments before the hospital staff went frantically into high gear in an effort to save them. Often they found their spiritual bodies going through a dark tunnel and emerging into a dazzling white light, so brilliant it should have blinded them, but seemed instead to be personified and to emanate love.

Some spoke of seeing a "Being of Light" which seemed to lovingly communicate without speaking, sometimes asking them non-judgmentally what they had done with their lives. Sometimes there followed a quick review of their lives like a newsreel movie presentation. Many were also welcomed and warmly greeted by deceased relatives and friends. Almost all spoke of a glorious, all-encompassing feeling of peace and happiness while there.

Then, for some strange, mystical reason, these "clinically dead" persons returned to their earthly bodies to begin anew their earthly lives. Sometimes, because of family obligations, the patients felt they must return, but most of them did not want to leave the beautiful new place they had found. They returned reluctantly. Afterwards, they felt their experience was so fantastic they hesitated to talk about it.

Dr. Moody's deep interest in these special experiences was first sparked at age 20 as a graduate student of philosophy at the University of Virginia when a professor related the story of a young soldier George Ritchie. This man had been pronounced dead of double pneumonia in an Army camp hospital in Texas during World War II and then, incredibly, was resuscitated more than nine minutes after being declared dead! During those nine minutes, Ritchie went through a series of experiences similar to, but even more dramatic than, the ones just described.[1]

A few months later Moody heard this same soldier - now George Ritchie, M.D., a highly respected physician and practicing psychiatrist in Moody's own college community of Charlottesville, Virginia - vividly describe his almost ineffable experience to a group of students.

Like the rest of the young audience, Moody was overwhelmed by Dr. Ritchie's revelation and equally impressed by his courage. That a successful physician would dare to publicly take the risk of admitting to having experienced a glimpse of the afterlife while clinically dead was an act of extraordinary valor in 1966.

Although he didn't realize it at the time, hearing Dr. Ritchie's testimony changed the course of Moody's life. A year after he completed his Ph.D. in philosophy in 1969 he was again "overwhelmed," to use his own words, to learn of another NDE almost exactly like Dr. Ritchie's.

By the time he entered medical school in 1972, he had collected eight such NDE case studies, and while attending medical school came upon many more. Eventually he had 150 cases which he studied carefully; with 50 of these he personally conducted interviews and then analyzed his findings. The result was his book, *Life After Life*, which with almost no advertising and little publicity, sold over 85,000 copies its first year and has subsequently become an international best-seller that has been read by millions.[2] Not surprisingly, the book was dedicated "to George Ritchie, M.D. and through him to the One whom he suggested."

In summarizing the research of his 150 NDE cases Dr. Moody quickly recognized the necessity of not drawing broad conclusions from the observations of only a few people. Despite the impressive and striking similarities in the general patterns, at the same time there were a number of variations in perception. For example, though many went through a tunnel, others talked of a void, a cave, a valley, or simply darkness while others had no experiences of this sort at all. Many met relatives and friends, but some did not. While some communicated with "Being of Light," others did not.

Among those who did communicate with a "Being of Light," some Christians interpreted it as God or Christ, some Jews as an angel, and many others as simply an inexplicable being of overpowering love.

A few cases were "clinically dead" and out of their physical bodies only long enough to witness the medical team desperately trying to revive them yet, quite incredibly, they reported the resuscitation procedure accurately on their return to earthly life. Some had no memory of anything during their period of physical death.

A subsequent Gallup Poll in 1981 surveying American attitudes regarding death and immortality, published in George Gallup's book, *Adventures in Immortality*, revealed that nearly eight million living Americans had near-death experiences similar to those Dr. Moody reported. Many of them spoke in wonder and awe of these episodes as "unforgettable" and "almost inexpressible."[3]

Here is the essence of a few of their cases:
   - In one particular case, the NDE survivor had a bad reaction
   to a local anesthetic and suffered a respiratory arrest. He
   ceased breathing. Suddenly he found himself going through

a black vacuum at super speed. He compared it to a tunnel. He also felt as though he was on a roller coaster train at an amusement park going through this tunnel at a break-neck speed.[4]

- In another case, after zooming through the tunnel and suddenly coming out into a beautiful light, the patient was warmly greeted by his grandmother and a girl he had known when he was in high school plus a number of relatives and friends. It was like a homecoming and they were there to welcome him. He said everything seemed to be so light and beautiful; he called it a truly glorious moment![5]

- Yet another NDE survivor told of being in a crystal clear light - the most illuminating white light he had ever seen - bright and radiant and beautiful - yet it didn't hurt his eyes. Then this light all about him seemed to take on a special identity; he called it a light of perfect understanding and love. The light seemed to say to him that he should go back and complete his life. All during this time, he felt surrounded with overwhelming love and compassion.[6]

- Still another NDE survivor related how he had experienced this wonderful light, and how the light had communicated with him - not in spoken words, but soul to soul - simply asking him what he had done that was worthwhile with his life. He found himself back in his early childhood, walking through each year of his life up to the present. These flashbacks were in color, three dimensional, as real as life itself. Each flashback seemed to be trying to show him

139

something...the importance of love...of trying to do one's best for others as well as yourself. When the flashbacks showed times where he had been selfish, the light did not accuse him but simply indicated to him how he could learn from such incidents. He felt he was actually living through these scenes, not just watching them. It all seemed to take less than five minutes and probably more than thirty seconds, but he had no idea of how to estimate the time.[7]

- Another patient related how ever since surviving his near-death experience, two thoughts had constantly dominated his mind - what had he done and not done with his life thus far, and what should he do with his life now that he'd been given a second chance... He now tried to do things that had more meaning than before, things that made his mind and soul feel better. He now tried much harder not to be biased and judgmental about people. Above all, he wanted to do things because they were good, not just because they benefitted him.[8]

- Three years after his near-death experience, another survivor testified - as did many others - that his minutes beyond death prior to his return were still as vivid as when they first happened to him and said it was a huge difference in his life. Even so, he admitted he didn't talk about it much. He'd confided in his wife, his brother and his minister - and now Dr. Moody - but it wasn't easy to explain what he'd been through without seeming to brag. But there was one thing he was certain of after the experience - there was one thing he didn't have any doubts about anymore - *he knew there was life after death!*[9]

Moving as these much abbreviated abstracts are, they cannot convey the full depth of feeling expressed by these people in Dr. Moody's wonderful book - it is as though you have entered a new world - which indeed you have. As Dr. Moody noted, "Their vision left them with new goals, new moral principles and a renewed determination to try to live in accordance with them, but with no feelings of instantaneous salvation or of moral infallibility."[10] And most striking of all, *"In one form or another, almost every person has expressed to me the thought that he or she is no longer afraid of death!"*[11]

Without bothering to read *Life after Life,* certain conservative clergy rejected his book and the phenomenon of the near-death experience as the satanic work of evil demons, according to Dr. Moody. On the other hand, a great many Christian clergy of differing denominations who took the time to read his book were enthralled by his findings and warmly applauded his work. Some were so enthusiastic that they invited him to speak to their congregations.[12]

Dr. Moody's book, so aptly named *Life after Life*, was obviously a book whose time had come. To thousands of his readers Dr. Moody's careful research and analysis became a major breakthrough in the search for proof of human survival after death providing fresh insights on the near-death experience.

However, a number of medical doctors and psychiatrists who had never heard of the near-death experience totally rejected the concept. Despite the authenticated cases of near-death experience presented in his book, a large segment of the medical profession still refused to believe there was any reality to the alleged phenomenon.[13]

Others, however, if they took the time to read Moody's book, were tentatively convinced that such things could occur though they rejected any metaphysical inference, believing that the near-death experience would one day be medically explained. Some gave no credence to his so-called "evidential" material because he relied almost entirely on anecdotal reports. Since some people lie or misremember, or misinterpret, or have delusions or hallucinations, especially under stress, anecdotal reports are not considered admissable scientific evidence.

On the other hand, a number of doctors accepted the phenomenon as a confirmation of their own religious faith even as Moody had done. In his book he frankly admitted that he accepted the idea of life after death as a matter of religious faith, but he also believed the phenomenon he had been examinng - the near-death experience - was a manifestation of life.[14]

Other doctors had their interest kindled in the NDE and began collecting reports of such cases. Their scientific curiosity had been aroused just as Moody's had been ten years prior.

A very small number of doctors who had personally had a NDE readily acknowledged to Dr. Moody the truth of his research findings. One such doctor ruefully confessed that as a scientist he would never have belived such a thing could happen - but having personally experienced it, he had to admit *it really did happen.*[15]

Young Dr. Moody, only 31 years old at that time, was undaunted by the mixed reactions to his book. Looking back on the attacks to which he had been subjected by some of his medical colleagues, he now concludes it was good to have skeptics around - for many who tried to prove him wrong ended up becoming believers themselves.[16]

Moody made no large claims for his study - he simply presented his findings as accurately as he could analyze them. When his first book came out in 1975 he disclaimed that he was making a case for survival after death. He frankly acknowledged that he was left not with conclusions or proof, but with something less definite - feelings, questions, puzzling facts to be explained - some of them seemingly unexplainable.[17]

Still, despite his disclaimer, he felt bound to report that the near-death experiences of the people he interviewed *were very real events to these people* and through his association with them, *these experiences became very real events to him.*[18]

But he was not satisfied with what he had learned and how little he really knew. He wanted to know more, much more! As he said at the close of his remarkable book, "What we learn about death may make an important difference in the way we live our lives. If experiences of the type which I have discussed are real, they have profound implications for what everyone of us is doing with his or her life. We cannot fully understand this life until we catch a glimpse of what lies beyond."[19]

In essence Dr. Moody's book was an eloquent call for much more research into what the near-death experience might be telling us about life *after* life!

In 1977, Dr. Kenneth Ring, a brilliant young professor of psychology at the University of Connecticut in Storrs, read Dr. Moody's book and was inspired by it. However, he felt that a more scientifically structured study would strengthen Moody's findings.

He sought out 102 near-death survivors for his research. Using a standardized questionnaire which he developed for defining and characterizing the near-death experience, he conducted interviews with 74

143

of these survivors; the remainder were conducted by a carefully trained graduate assistant.

Based on his meticulous research, here in essence are some of Dr. Ring's basic insights:

1.Those cases who came closest to death or were clinically dead, just as Moody's cases reported, told of being outside of their bodies, of moving through a void or dark tunnel toward a luminous light, of meeting with departed relatives and friends, of having a feeling of great comfort and bliss and of being surrounded by compassionate love, a feeling so beautiful they longed to remain, and when they returned to the "earthly" realm, were affected by this feeling the rest of their lives.[20]

2. No one type of person was especially likely to have this experience. It cut across race, gender, age, education, marital status, and social class.[21]

3. Religious orientation was not a fact affecting either the likelihood or the depth of the near-death experience. An atheist was as likely to have one as was a devoutly religious person.[22]

4. Regardless of their prior attitudes - whether skeptical or deeply religious - and regardless of the many variations in religious belief and degrees of skepticism from tolerant disbelief to outspoken atheism - most of these people were convinced that they had been in the presence of some

supreme and loving power and had a glimpse of a life yet to come.[23]

5. Drugs, anesthesia and medication did not seem to be a factor in inducing these impressions and exquisite feelings of the NDE. Indeed, drugs and anesthesia seemed to be more likely to cause a person to forget such a near-death experience.[24]

6. He definitely concluded NDEs were not hallucinations since hallucinations are rambling, unconnected, often unintelligible and vary widely, whereas NDEs all tend to have similar elements of a clear, connected pattern.[25]

7. Based on the information of those who had reported such incidents, the moment of death was often one of unparalleled beauty, peace and comfort - a feeling of total love and total acceptance. This was possible even for those involved in horrible accidents in which they suffered very serious injuries. Ring found there was a tremendous comfort potential in this information for people who were facing death.[26]

8. After going through a near-death experience, people reported a loss of fear of death as well as a greater appreciation of life. They also reported stronger feelings of self-acceptance and a greater concern and sense of caring for other people. They had less interest in material things for their own sake. Many tended to become more spiritual - though not necessarily more involved in organized religion.[27]

145

9. Almost all who experienced the NDE found their lives transformed and a change in their attitudes and values, and in their inclination to love and to help others. Ring was convinced that these were absolutely authentic experiences[28] and noted that since returning, many of them had occasion to think about 'what might have been.' And their subsequent lives were powerful testimony to our common ability to live more deeply, more appreciatively, more lovingly, and more spiritually.[29]

Dr. Ring's searching, two-year inquiry resulted in a splendid book, *Life at Death: A Scientific Investigation of the Near-Death Experience* (1980). As his subtitle indicated, it was a truly scientific investigation; his carefully designed research study adhered to the strict, statistical, empirical method that learned scientific societies applaud. Yet his book was by no means as dull as such academic restrictions make it sound; it is a highly readable and enthralling account of an adventurous quest because, like Moody, he is an enthusiastic human being who became inspired by the mystery and larger meaning of the near-death experience.

His book features an introduction by Dr. Moody generously applauding Ring and his associates for their much higher level of systematization. In a later book praising Dr. Ring's research, Moody said this study legitimatized his work by taking the scientific step, noting that everyone now doing NDE research uses Dr. Ring's work as a reference and standard for their methodology.[30] As *Newsday* wrote, "with the publication of *Life at Death*, there can be no question that a common set of near-death phenomena does exist."[31]

Dr. Ring's research helped greatly to more sharply define and further clarify the small but awesome body of knowledge we are still in process of gathering about this mysterious phenomenon.

In 1984 Dr. Ring caused a new flurry of excitement in the NDE realm when his second book, *Heading Toward Omega: In Search of the Meaning of the Near Death Experience,* appeared. In this heartening, more philosophical study, through detailed interviews with about a hundred near-death survivors he sought to determine how the NDE had affected their lives. His findings substantiated Moody's earlier conclusions: that a major change takes place in the lives of those who experience the NDE and that it is a powerful catalyst for spiritual awakening.

Dr. Elisabeth Kubler-Ross, physician, psychiatrist and thanatolgist, author of the landmark books *Of Death and Dying* (1970) and *Death - the Final Stage of Growth* (1975), almost singlehandedly brought about in our hospitals a revolution of mercy, honesty and sensitivity in the treatment of the terminally ill. She wrote an eloquent "Foreword" to Ring's second book as she had done for Moody's first.

Her first-hand treatment of thousands of terminally ill hospital patients, many of whom had NDEs and told her about them, gave her an immediate understanding of what Moody and Ring were talking about. In *Heading Toward Omega* she told of the occasion when she "was allowed to experience and become part of that light which so many people try to explain in words. Anyone who has been blessed enough to see this light will never again be afraid to die. The unconditional love, the understanding and compassion, in the presence of this light are beyond any human description. Perhaps the greatest contribution of Kenneth's new book is, it tries to comprehend the ensuing changes persons undergo once they have been in the presence of this light. It is a spiritual, sacred experience which leaves the person profoundly transformed. The near-death experience also gives new dimensions to living and to the understanding of human life and purpose."[32]

147

Ring's in-depth research into 100 near-death cases revealed that almost universally they became more selfless, more caring and more spiritual human beings. The goodness within their spirits seemed to have been ignited by the light and love they witnessed, their consciousness raised to a higher plane and they remained transformed for the rest of their lives. Here are examples of life-transformation brought about by NDEs as recorded by Dr. Ring:

1. One survivor, a recovered alcoholic who nearly died of liver failure, felt he had become an entirely different person since his near-death experience. Whereas he had been miserable and self-destructive before that experience, he was now serene, calm, happy and lived every 24 hours trying to do just little bit for his fellow human beings even if not more than a smile to cheer up some unhappy looking person.[33]

2. Another survivor, a woman who had attempted suicide, said that ever since her NDE, people described her as being on "a high in life," And they were right, she felt, because she was thankful for every new day God gave her and she never took a single minute of her life for granted. There just weren't words to express the change in her, she said, but she was sure of one thing; she felt a peace inside herself that remained with her always now and it had the strangest calming effect on her.[34]

3. Referring to her encounter with the light, another NDE survivor described the light as accepting, forgiving and completely non-judgmental, and it gave her a sense of total security beyond anything she had ever known. She called it

perfection - total, unconditional love. Regarding the effect of this experience upon her sense of herself, she said she had learned to accept herself as she was - probably the greatest lesson she had ever learned after a difficult, life-long struggle. It was then she decided that if the light and the presence could accept her with all her weaknesses and faults, then she had to be an OK person.[35]

4. Still another survivor testified to a new understanding of life and love following her NDE. Her whole being had been transformed by her experience, she said, and now her life was one of calmness and love. She had gained a new awareness of the true value of existence and of the connectedness she had with every other living thing. She felt awed now by everything that happened to her. People didn't seem to realize, she said, that heaven was really right here if you just opened your eyes and mind and heart to what was really going on.[36]

5. After her near-death experience, this particular survivor noticed that she seemed to reach out and touch people more. And she also observed that she somehow seemed to make people feel better. Whenever there was a family problem, everyone seemed to turn to her. She said she seemed to have more insight into people now. And because she was much more sensitive to the pain in their eyes, it was difficult for her to lose her temper anymore. She realized now what really counted was one's relationships to one's fellow human beings. Love was the answer - indeed love was the answer to everything![37]

6. Many other survivors similarly felt a new love for people following their NDEs. One was surprised to find it was much easier since his NDE to love everybody in a way had never felt before.[38] Yet another said simply that since his near-death experience he loved people in a warm and wonderful way that he had never felt in the past, and found himself wishing he could help everyone who needed help.[39]

These brief summaries convey only a fraction of the impact of the full testimony of the near-death survivors contained in Dr. Ring's *Heading Toward Omega*. His additional evidence adds new dimensions and further mystery to the near-death experience and the signals it seems to be sending us regarding our hopes for beautiful life and all-encompassing love beyond death.

Another frontline researcher who played an important role in establishing the validity and reality of the near-death experience was Dr. Michael B. Sabom, a cardiologist in private practice in Atlanta, Georgia.

In 1977, while in cardiovascular training at the University of Florida, he read Dr. Moody's book and found it fascinating. Because he had not yet personally encountered any NDE cases, he couldn't quite believe they actually existed. Then he casually asked a number of his patients and was amazed at how many had personally undergone an NDE. He was further amazed to discover that these experiences had been happening to people whom he and his colleagues had been taking care. Obviously these experiences were so fantastic the patients hesitated to talk about them; they were fearful no one would believe them - or worse still, that they might be classified as having "gone off the deep end" and be sent to the psycho ward.[40]

The challenge of Dr. Moody's book, plus these stories from his patients, inspired Dr. Sabom to search out the full facts in the perfect laboratory - the hospital in which he was working. Dr. Sabom was struck with stories from 32 of these NDE cases who had out-of-body experiences during the period they were clinically dead. These patients testified that rising above their conscious bodies, sometimes near the ceiling, they actually watched the doctor and medical team frantically performing their resuscitation procedures.

When he checked out these stories, Dr. Sabom found that some of the patients could tell him in detail, in the correct sequence, exactly what had happened to their bodies on the operating table. One man described how he floated above his body and watched the operating team at work. He described the instruments, how the heart looked, and the procedure itself. Dr. Sabom was surprised at his detailed description for there was nothing in the patients's background to indicate he had picked up this medical knowledge elsewhere. In another case, a man's heart had stopped beating for four to five minutes, and he described - exactly - what went on during that time. To Dr. Sabom this was the strongest evidence that these were not hallucinations or fantasies. As Sabom saw it, there was something going on in these cases that couldn't be explained in traditional ways.[41]

Dr. Sabom later compared their descriptions of the resuscitation procedure with the "educated guesses" of 25 medically savvy patients about what happens when a doctor and medical team tries to get the heart started again. 23 of the 25 patients in the outside group made major mistakes in describing what went on during resuscitation; by contrast, every one of the 32 near-death patients described exactly the resuscitation procedure! Dr. Sabom took this as strong evidence - as did Dr. Moody when he later examined the data - that these people were actually outside their bodies, looking down and observing the exact procedure during the

151

period when they were clinically dead.[42]

Dr. Sabom's in-depth NDE study of 120 hospital patients was published in his book, *Recollections of Death; A Medical Investigation*, (1982) which like Ring's research, verified Dr. Moody's findings.[43] Not surprisingly, like Drs. Moody and Ring, Dr. Sabom became inspired by the mystery and larger meaning of the near-death experience.

He wrote: "My personal reaction to these events is not so much a 'scientifically weighted' response as it is a keenly felt identification with the tears of joy and sorrow that have accompanied the unfolding of many of these stories. My involvement in the lives and deaths of the people in this book has made me humble to the ways of the universe, much like Albert Einstein, who once wrote:

> Everyone who is seriously involved in the pursuit of science becomes convinced that a Spirit is manifest in the Laws of the Universe - a Spirit vastly superior to that of man, and one in the face of which we, with our modest powers, must feel humble.[44]

For it is precisely this 'Spirit' which has been acknowledge time and time again by the majority of those encountering an NDE... And it is precisely this 'Spirit' which seems to live on in the lives of those who were touched by some ineffable truth encountered face to face at death's closest moments."[45]

By mid-1981, Dr. Fred Schoonmaker, Director of Cardiovascular Services at St. Luke's Hospital of Denver, had amassed medical records and case histories of 2,300 patients who came close to death. He found *more than 1400 cases or over 60% of those reported had near-death experiences similar to those in Moody's, Ring's and Sabom's studies.*[46]

Dr. Melvin Morse, presently a pediatrician in Seattle, Washington, did near-death studies of children while working for Airlift Northwest. Because the airlift rescued emergency patients for an Idaho hospital he found himself dealing with scores of resuscitated children. Becoming curious about the NDE phenomenon, with the hospital's permission, he interviewed every child survivor of cardiac arrest over a 10 year period.

His conclusion: this "innocent" population, with far less exposure to religious and cultural conditioning than adults, nevertheless had near-death experiences similar to their elders. They went down tunnels, viewed their bodies from outside themselves, saw beings of light and had virtually identical experiences to the adults.

He noted the common sense attitude of the children about their near-death experiences. Unlike many adults, they weren't overawed and didn't think this was the most powerful event in their lives. *They were very realistic and simply took it as a matter of course that this was what happened when you died.*[47]

Dr. Bruce Greyson, while assistant professor of psychiatry at the University of Michigan, studied more than 150 near-death cases in the Michigan area. His conclusions corroborated those of Moody, Ring and Sabom.

He was particularly interested in attempted suicides and discovered that those suicide survivors who had also encountered a near-death experience came out of them with a real sense of purpose in their lives. Although death was no longer fearful, life became more meaningful.[48]

This, also, was precisely Moody's finding. He found they came back from their experience feeling they had learned they had a purpose to fulfill here in life. They returned with a serious, dedicated attitude toward life and living.[49]

In recent years as a doctor of emergency psychiatry at the University of Connecticut, Dr. Greyson has dealt with suicides almost daily. His research there has shown a most revealing fact: a high percentage of those suicide survivors who have not experienced the NDE did attempt suicide again. By contrast, those suicide survivors who had undergone an NDE, almost never attempt such a self-inflicted terminal departure a second time.[50]

This too, validated Moody's findings. No one he interviewed had ever sought a repeat performance of taking their own life.[51] The message from the heart of the universe of being loved with a totally non-judgmental affection, so healed these people, so restored their self-esteem, that never again would they take the path of self-destruction.

The findings of Drs. Ring, Sabom, Schoonmaker, Morse and Greyson fully substantiate the truth and reality of Dr. Moody's pioneer research in 1975. It is obvious that he didn't just invent the 150 NDE cases about which he wrote so eloquently. It is now quite clear that his initial findings - which he courageously published at great risk to his professional status - were the ground-breaking discoveries of an inspired young scientist.

As Moody himself wrote, "near death experiences intrigue us because they are the most tangible proof of spiritual existence that can be found. They are truly the light at the end of the tunnel."[52]

The career of Raymond Moody Jr. did not stop with publication of his first book, *Life After Life*. From the moment his book was published his life would never be the same. He quickly came to realize that he had written about an enormously popular subject and that almost everyone seemed to be interested in solving humankind's most perplexing mystery - its life and love beyond death.[53] Consequently, he increased his intensive research, spoke to thousands from the lecture platform, and reached out to millions via radio and TV regarding the near-death experience.

In 1977 he wrote an admirable sequel, *Reflections on Life After Life*. In 1988 in writing *The Light Beyond* he summarized what he had learned from having personally interviewed over 1,000 near-death experiences and having been advisor, consultant or acquaintance of almost everyone involved in research into the NDE.

To the question: "Are NDEs evidence of life after life?" he replies with a resounding, "Yes!" At the same time he does not claim this on what might be called "firm scientific proof."

He explains it this way: "After 22 years of looking at the near-death experience, I think there isn't enough scientific proof to show conclusively that there is life after death. But that means *scientific* proof. Matters of the heart are different. They do not require a strictly scientific view of the world. Researchers like myself use what we would describe as *educated analysis. Based on such examination, I am convinced that NDErs do get a glimpse of the beyond, a brief passage into a whole other reality.* "[54]

He cites the case of Dr. Carl Gustav Jung, one of the world's greatest psycho-therapists, who had his own dear-death experience during a heart attack in 1944. Afterwards he wrote, "What happens after death is so unspeakably glorious that our imaginations and our feelings do not suffice to form even an approximate conception of it!"[55]

Jung's statement brings to mind the vision of life after death by the great Jewish philosopher, theologian and physician, Moses Maimonides, when he said, "There is no way at all for us in this world to know or comprehend the great goodness which the soul experiences in the world to come...*That good is great beyond all our understanding and incomparable beyond all our imagination!*"[56]

Some Personal Psychic Experiences
and Subjective Spiritual Reflections.
Our Death Is Our Rebirth into a
New Dimension of More Beautiful
Love! Our Greatest Adventures
Still Lie Ahead!

During World War II, when my ambulance was bombed in the Egyptian Desert, something quite unbelievable happened!

In the long, hot summer of 1942 Field Marshall Rommel and his crack Afrika Corp were less than 60 miles from Alexandria's suburbs frantically trying to break through the British El Alamein line - with plans to then race on with lightning speed to the Suez Canal - to be immediately followed by a blitzkrieg take-over of the whole Middle East. Among Rommel's more frenetic moves to prepare for that breakthrough were frequent night attacks and daily bombings of everything in sight along the battle-front. Waves of 20 to 50 Stukas would dive-bomb us regularly, sometimes two or three times a day.

One horrendous, chaotic afternoon, I had picked up a wounded soldier from a regimental aid post near the frontline and was coming back to a temporary medical aid dressing station which had been set up to service the many wounded from the previous night's attack. Just as I drove up, I heard and then saw a horde of planes coming toward us. I spotted some slit trenches to the rear of my vehicle and got out my wounded patient, put him in one and then got in one myself. Already the planes were overhead and the anti-aircraft fire was pounding, filling the

157

sky with white spurts of smoke. To the left and right explosions shattered the air and mushrooms of dust and fire rose where bombs hit the earth.

Then, directly above me, a plane dove down. I did not look up to see it above me, my face was in the sand, but I could tell by the screech of the plane, the whistle of the wings cutting the air and the savage drive

of the plane's big engine that it was charging to the ground. The bombs were released with an ear-breaking scream, so loud it seemed to cut into my flesh. I shrank deeper into the earth as the scream tore through me and the bombs zoomed down on me. I lay there and waited, my feelings now beyond fear, accepting the inevitable. This was it. This was the finish! In a second it would all be over as I'd be torn to bits too small for burial.

Then the bombs hit, one five yards away, another fifteen, the whole earth shook about me, dirt from the sides of my slit trench moved in on me, pieces of shrapnel hit the walls of my trench and I waited for the steel to drive through my flesh. I waited for death.

Next it was all whirling dust and sound about me, then only dust. I could hardly believe I was still alive for by every right I should have been dead. As I lay in my trench, covered with dust and half buried with sand, I could not help feeling that somehow I had been saved.

Then the planes flew off as swiftly as they had come. On the ground half a dozen vehicles were burning or wrecked including my ambulance and a score or more of men lay wounded, some for the second time.

I scrambled out of my trench, grateful beyond words just to be alive. Though still half dazed from the impact of those screaming bombs, I pulled my patient out of his trench, got him medical help and then went on helping the other wounded men until all were taken care of. Later at dusk, I sat alone in my wrecked ambulance, waiting for the salvage crew to haul it back to their shop miles behind the frontline. I simply stared ahead of me, too grateful for being alive to even think thoughts. Though devoid of reason, my state was not one of utter misery, for I found myself flooded with a surging warmth, an all-encompassing consciousness. I still lived, still breathed, still could feel air in my lungs, sense flesh on my bones, still saw with my eyes, felt life in my groins and though the bomb still screamed in my ears, I could still hear. I spoke aloud, just to make sure. "Dave Hyatt," I said, and my name came back to me. My ears were all right. What a privilege to still be alive!

Gradually the dusk grew greyer, and in the sightlessness of the desert dusk, I sought for some means of distracting my mind from the scream of the bombs that still churned in my head. I opened the glove compartment beside the wrecked dashboard. There, dust-covered with a few small pieces of shrapnel cutting into it, was my *Book of Psalms*. Though I'd rarely found time to read it, I liked having it there; it had been a gift of a dear lady friend.

I reached for the small, black volume and opened it. Then I abruptly stiffened and a chill ran down my spine. *"Yea, though I walk through the valley of the shadow of death, I shall fear no evil, for Thou art with me,"*[1] were the first words I read. I re-read the words, shocked and amazed. Was it just a coincidence, that the events of that day linked so precisely with these words now before me?

The scream of the bombs still tore at my eardrums - over and over again the bombs came down within me, breaking the stillness of the desert around me, now dusky grey, vast and infinite, the sands stretching beyond sight to the edge of the oncoming night. Perhaps it *was* coincidence - the bombing and those words - but alone in this wasteland in a bombed ambulance, alive, when by all rights I should have been dead, I found it more logical to believe I'd been saved.

"Yea, though I walk through the valley of the shadow of death, I shall fear no evil, for Thou art with me," I read once more, and out of gratitude and humility for the privilege of living, I deeply believed those words.

Another time I got lost in the desert and was mystically guided to where I had to go. It was another remarkable incident for which I have no explanation except, "Thank God!"

There is no way to convey to you the terrible ache in your throat and heart when you're lost in the desert in the darkness of the night during an attack. You have four horribly wounded soldiers aboard in your ambulance and you have no idea where the Casualty Clearing Station is.

When your ambulance was loaded with these four wounded men at an Advanced Dressing Station near the front, you were told the Casualty Clearing Station should be north-north-east about three miles unless it had to move to get out of shelling range. You head north-north-east, guided by the North Star. You dare not turn on your lights - that would be suicide - your only light for driving is the light of the stars and a thin sickle moon.

You drive and drive and there is no life about you - only sand, wasteland and wreckage of past battles - and sand and more sand. You drive three miles, then four, then five. Finally you begin to numbly realize that if you keep on driving you could wind up in the middle of the desert by morning with four men slowly bleeding to death in the back of your vehicle.

Feeling hopelessly lost, you stop and get out for a moment just to calm your anxiety. All you can see in the starlight are vast stretches of sand and all you can hear is the low moaning of the wounded in your ambulance; even under morphine they are still in anguish and you feel

160

their pain with them. You stand beside your ambulance peering across the wasteland and pray inwardly as you have never prayed before: "Dear God, lead me to the medical aid station. Help me to find it for the sake of these men!"

You listen for guidance and then get back behind the wheel and start driving again - not north-north-east but straight east, because some inner voice directed you to now head east.

You drive for half a mile, then you suddenly see a truck's shadow in the darkness. You drive up to it and find two men in sleeping bags under the truck.

"Can you tell me where the medical aid station is?"

"We're part of it," one of them tells me. "Just keep going the way you're heading about a quarter of a kilometer and you'll run into the main medical and surgical receiving."

Only minutes later an orderly and I carried the stretchers of the wounded men into the big canvas medical and surgical tent which was lit inside by gasoline lanterns over the surgical tables. A young surgeon quickly, but carefully examined each of the patients, then said to me, "It's good you got them here when you did. They'll all require surgery, but they'll be all right. They'll make it fine now."

"Thank God," I said simply.

Never in my life did I rejoice and thank God as I did at that moment. Without expressing it aloud, from the utmost depth of my heart and soul I also thanked His unseen guardian messenger who had mystically directed me when lost in the desert, had told me to turn from north-north-east to east and had miraculously saved those four wounded men.

Still another personal psychic experience which remains vividly etched in my memory happened in January of 1944.

Nine months after my father died he paid me an unexpected visit.

As a newly appointed U.S. junior naval officer, I was temporarily stationed at St. Simons Island, Georgia for intensive training in the radar direction of fighter planes. One evening around 10 o'clock, he quietly appeared in my room.

I was stretched on my bed, dog-tired from the day's rigorous, non-stop training activities and had closed my eyes, expecting to immediately drop off to sleep. Suddenly I saw the image of my dad in my mind - as real and alive as though he were actually in the room. It was like a dream, only I was still awake.

"Hyuh, Dave," he said, smiling warmly, "I thought I'd drop in on you just to let you know I am still alive."

He was deeply tanned, tall, lean and handsome in one of his usual graceful, brown suits; his silver grey-blue eyes were full of light. He looked wonderful.

"My God - Dad!" I exclaimed. "Is it really you?"

He smiled, amused. "Yes, it's me all right, Dave. You thought I died back last April, didn't you? Well, in the words of Mark Twain, the reports of my death are highly exaggerated."

The image of him was so clear it was like life-size color television. I wasn't asleep, I was totally conscious and in my mind's eyes, I clearly saw him. I talked with him as a medium sees and converses with someone from the next dimension while in a trance - but unlike a medium, I was not in trance, nor was I unconscious.

"Obviously Mark Twain was right about you," I said. I couldn't help but smile at his lighthearted, cavalier comments which were so typical of him. "You really look terrific."

He sat down on the edge of my bed. "Well, Dave, I sure got a surprise after the doctors declared I was dead. I'd always thought death meant the end of one's life." There was a twinkle in his eyes. "You know you people on earth are a lot deader than we are."

I laughed. I'd never heard or read of anyone saying that before. "Thanks a lot," I responded wryly.

Dad was a great joker, always making quips, always looking for humor in everything. He had a particularly ironical sense of humor about death. "Do you remember that old gag I used to pull - I'm sure I must have cribbed it from Jack Benny or Fred Allen or some other comedian. Whenever things got too serious, I used to say menacingly, 'Listen you buzzards, I warn you - *not one of you will ever get out of this world alive!*'"

I laughed again. "I remember that old cornball of yours, I always thought you made it up."

"But you know, Dave, that joke isn't funny to me anymore. In fact, it isn't even true. *Everyone* gets out of this world alive - not only alive, but more alive than ever before. We're on a much higher frequency on the Other Side - we're much more sensitive, much more aware and much more conscious of everything about us than we ever were on earth. That's one of the many dividends of our life in the next dimension to which you can really look forward."

Then he looked at me intently. "I'm really sorry I wasn't around to greet you when you got back last April."

"You couldn't have been sorrier than I was," I answered. "Your checking out before I ever got home was really a low blow, Dad."

He had passed out suddenly, while at work in his office in Terre Haute, Indiana one April morning in 1943. He was rushed to the hospital and five days later, still unconscious, died of encephalitis - an infection and inflammation of the outer lining of the brain caused by, of all things, a germ-carrying mosquito's bite.

163

"It was a weird way to go," he commented matter-of-factly, "but obviously my time had come. I'm just grateful that it was me that was taken and not you, Dave."

"Well, you turned my homecoming into a wake, Dad. The first news I heard on arriving in New York was that you had just died. It was one of the worst days of my life."

"Hell, you should have celebrated!" he came back merrily. "Not because you were rid of me - although that might be a good reason - but because I've moved on to a larger, more exciting life. The way I see it now, for nearly everyone who has led a half-way decent life, death should be a celebration. You lose nothing in death but your physical body - and you leave behind all your old ailments and past, stupid mistakes and other dammed baggage - and you bring with you everything you've ever learned - nothing of value is ever lost. Our moving to the next plane is just a great opportunity for personal growth and development."

"But 53 is just too damned young to die!" I said.

"Age 18 and 20 and 25 is even more so!" he responded almost fiercely. "I'm afraid we earthlings have a terrible habit of killing off our young. Thank God in our family at least, my number came up before yours."

He paused for a moment looking into my eyes with deep intensity, "I never was very good at expressing my real feelings, Dave, except when I got sore and then all hell broke loose. But I want you to know how proud I am of what you did overseas. Not only as an ambulance driver, but as a war correspondent. Those articles you wrote were terrific! Not many young men of 26 get a full column by-lined spread in *The New York Times* and 120 other newspapers the way you did."

"That was just luck, Dad. I just happened to be at Tobruk when the retreat broke and at El Alamein when that line was set up and held."

164

Long before I had arrived in Suez, Dad was already proud of my going overseas. At the time I enlisted - before Pearl Harbor - I was sure about only one thing above all - that Hitler and the Nazis had to be stopped. I couldn't stand what Hitler was doing to the Jews and everyone else who believed in freedom. While the U.S. was play a "wait-it-out" game of neutrality, it seemed to me that Great Britain was fighting our war.

When I learned that the American Field Service was sending ambulances and enlisting volunteers to drive them for the British for the British 8th Army in North Africa - even though you had to agree to serve without pay and I had no money - I signed up immediately. Somehow I knew it was something I was meant to do, and indeed, it changed my whole life.

To cover my incidental expenses for the first few months, I sold everything I owned for which there was any market - my two good suits, my record player, my records and my books; but my total assets only netted $200 in cash. To bring in a few more dollars for spending money, I saw John Wheeler of North American Newspaper Alliance before we sailed from New York City to Suez on the Egyptian steamer S.S. El Nil; he agreed to buy any articles I sent him, "provided the articles are any good."

As it turned out, the eight feature articles which I wrote from the back of my ambulance and airmailed back to Wheeler at $25 per article were syndicated all over the U.S. and kept me from being penniless during my many months in Egypt and Libya.

"Now that I'm over on the Other Side," Dad continued, "I've also got to admit that you were right about this business of death and a lot of the other metaphysical things we discussed before you went overseas. I now know that there's a Higher Power and that God and Love are one and same and these are the only things that matter in the whole damned

165

universe. Most of what we think is important when we're on earth - getting ahead, being successful, making it big in business or politics or in a profession, making a lot of money, achieving high rank - are just chaff that the wind blows away. What really counts is what you did for others - how much you loved beyond yourself - how much you really loved and how well!"

"I'm glad you said all this, Dad," I answered. I had never heard him speak in this manner; he had always been a humorously cynical disbeliever.

"We don't usually make this kind of a call, Dave, but as an ambulance driver you saw more than your share of death and then to have me drop off in the ridiculous way I departed, I thought it might help you to know that your metaphysics are on the right track - that there is no death and that all of your loved ones who have left this earth are alive and well and are often with you in spirit even though you can't see us or hear us."

"To hear you bear witness to all this from the Other Side - and you a life-long skeptic - is great news, Dad," I answered.

"Dave, I came back for just one very particular reason - to stop you from grieving about my so-called 'death,' I wasn't sure whether I'd be able to get through to you - but now that you see how alive I am, you can understand how pointless it is to grieve - it really makes it harder for us to do what we're meant to do."

"I'll remember that, Dad."

"Just remember from now on that we're not only still alive but more alive than we ever were before - so when you think about me, I want you to be happy for me, not mournful."

"From now on, Dad, that's a promise."

Just at that moment the "Lights Out" warning bell rang.

Dad jumped, "What the hell is that?"

"That's the Navy's childish way of making sure that its young officers in training get enough sleep."

"Well, I'd better get the hell out of here. I'll be damned if I want to wind up playing a wispy old ghost in a blackout here in front of you."

Again I couldn't help laughing. His sense of humor was irrepressible.

Then I asked, "Where will you go now, Dad?"

"To a lecture."

"About what?"

"About God - what else? All they do in the group I'm with is talk about God."

"How did you wind up in such a group?"

He shrugged. "I'm afraid I don't completely understand it, I'm told that like attracts like and that you wind up among people of your same level of spiritual development. So in a way, I guess I made my own choice."

"Well, there you are!" I countered, smiling, "You must be further developed than you thought you were."

"On the other hand," he came back, "maybe I'm just there because I'm so ignorant about the subject." Self-depreciating humor was one of Dad's specialties.

"But you just said you were with a group of your own choosing. It was up to you."

"That's right."

"So what are you grumbling about?"

He smiled at himself. "I guess it's just that they're all so advanced - they seem way beyond me, way over my head. And they're always so damned serious."

"Maybe they need someone like you to bring a little humor to the subject. You used to say God had to have the world's greatest sense of

167

humor as well as the most unbelievable patience to endure the stupidity of the human race."

Now he was smiling. "Maybe you're right. In any case, I can't believe God doesn't have a sense of humor, can you?"

"Well, maybe that's why you're there, Dad. Those lectures sound fascinating to me."

"Oh you'd love them, Dave. And unlike your father, you might even fully understand them."

The warning "Lights Out" bell rang a second time and Dad got up to go.

"Now I'm going to leave you, Dave, with this uplifting thought," he said solemnly, "Just remember that no matter what happens, things are bound to get better - for you'll never be deader than you are right now!"

A broad grin lit up his handsome face, "As always it was a joy to be with you," he said affectionately, "but don't tell anyone else you talked with me or they'll ship you off to the psycho ward!"

Then he said very quietly, with muted emotion, "God bless you, Dave." And as abruptly and suddenly as he came, he was gone. He didn't make an exit, nor walk to the door, he just was no longer there seeming to vanish into thin air.

Dad never again came to see me as he did at St. Simons Island, Georgia and never again did I experience such a visual psychic encounter with anyone else from the Other Side. Needless to say, I heeded Dad's warning so I would not wind up in the psycho ward.

I'll never know whether that visit with Dad was a psychic fact and living actuality - or the product of an over-active imagination - or the wistful, wishful dreaming of a lonely son in search of self-help therapy. But whether fact or fiction, his visit was so real that ever since that unforgettable night in January, 1944, I have felt inspired and strengthened by an inner faith that my Dad still lives in the next dimension; gallantly and with indomitable good humor, he sometimes guides me, helps me, from the Other Side.

Another memorable psychic experience occurred to me during the months of April to October of 1984 when I received some inspiring insights into life and love beyond death through *automatic writing*. This is one of the wondrous ways of communication between our world and the next whereby the sender from the Other Side writes through the hand and pen of an earthling receiver as was described in our chapter on Bert Terhune who used the hand and pen of Mrs. S___ to communicate with his beloved Anice.

It was through this same process that Frederic W. H. Myers, a co-founder and charismatic leader of the Society for Psychical Research of Great Britain, after his death communicated to us about life on the Other Side. These writings were authenticated by Sir Oliver Lodge as characteristic of his good friend Frederic.

During his lifetime Myers had been a distinguished Cambridge University poet, philosopher, classical scholar and lecturer, and the author of a landmark book of scholarly research on *Human Personality and Its Survival of Bodily Death*. In this book he originated the words and defined the pioneer concepts of "telepathy" and "subliminal consciousness." This monumental, two-volume, 1,361 page treatise, is still hailed as "unquestionably the most famous, most original and most important single work in psychical research."[2]

Thirty one years after his death, thanks to automatic writing, Myers contributed another mind-stretching book, *The Road to Immortality*

(1932), for which his good friend Sir Oliver Lodge wrote the Foreword. Utilizing the hand and pen of one of the world's most gifted psychics, Geraldine Cummins, Myers described life after death on the various planes beyond our realm.

In the Introduction to this book, Mrs. E. G. Gibbes, a long-time friend and colleague of Miss Cummins, explains the significance of automatic writing in the world of psychic phenomena:

> Automatic writing has been proved to be a genuine phenomenon in which the hand of the scribe writes matter of which he or she at times may have no conscious knowledge.....

> It is possible that certain people are "tuned in" to higher vibrations, and that, through such vibrations, the so-called dead may communicate again with the world they left.[3]

One morning in April of 1984, as I sat at my desk dreamily envisioning a book I hoped to write about the psychic realm which I was then fervently studying, my hand began to move and my pen began to write without any help from me. Strangely, as this happened, it was as though I wasn't there at all. I looked down and read what had been written: *Let us meet regularly at 10:30 or 11 a.m. and see if you can relax sufficiently to blank out your mind and clear a channel for our thoughts to come through to you as you are doing now.*

My mind immediately asked, "Who is doing this writing?" No sooner did this question flash through my head than my pen again began moving without help from me and quickly printed out the following:

We are your guides - your lifelong counselors. But who we are is unimportant. We applaud your contemplated book. We propose that you allow us to record through you our impressions of life in the next dimension. This may then lead you to find other sources of similar material with the view of presenting to your earthling brothers and sisters a clearer, more explicit picture of what life is like and how we operate in the next dimension.

There is, indeed, life after life on earth! And it can be beautiful, wonderful life if humankind wishes to make it so. We will try to describe for you such a life and what one must do to make it so. Goodbye and God bless you - until tomorrow.

The pen then abruptly stopped and no longer was there anyone there to move it except myself.

What followed over the next six months was a series of comments about life and love beyond death given to me through automatic writing, so appealing and uplifting that I am moved to present a few excerpts here of what was given me.

April 30, 1984:

In marriage on earth, ideally there is a melding of spirits, a melding of the hearts and minds of two people in love and through intercourse, a coupling and melding of two passionate bodies along with the melding of two hearts and minds and souls. And in this melding, the two people for a moment - if it is true love and not merely sexual gratification - become one, completely united, two lovers suddenly melded into one inseparable, beautiful love.

The same thing happens in the next dimension - we find our perfect soulmate and just as on earth you meld and couple through love into an exquisite, passionate expression of love that unites you, though two, as one - so can we in this next dimension meld with the person we love and totally immerse ourselves in his or her heart and mind and soul in an ecstatic

171

love that in intensity and oneness is beyond any earthly experience humankind has known. It is pure joy, pure ecstasy, pure feeling - the ultimate essence of a loving union because it is unencumbered by the veil of flesh. Our etheric bodies, being less 'solid,' being not of the flesh but of vibrations, can blend and meld even as the different sounds of music blend and meld to become a gorgeous and sublime symphony.

May 3:

It is the spirit that makes the human body the holy and sacred vessel of God that it is. The spirit is what lives on after death. It cannot be extinguished because it is energy, it is vibration, it is a part of the universe that is indestructible. And so when one dies, one's etheric body and one's mind still possess everything one learned on earth as one moves to the next dimension.

The wisdom you have gained, the experience, the joy of love and of loving God and of loving another special human being as a mate and rearing children and loving them very specially, as well as loving many other human beings as friends and relatives and business and community associates, is all a part of the earthly loving experience. You came into being upon your earth to learn about love. You then will graduate to the next dimension to learn more about love - to refine and expand your capacity to love and to nurture it and develop it as you would nourish and tenderly care for a garden of beautiful flowers.

July 29:

Most of our earthly lives are engaged in activities that are simply 'busy.' They are like games of chess or bridge or solitaire which simply serve to pass the time. Too often one's work is in the same category. It is simply passing one's time doing 'busy work' that has no meaning to the doer except that it brings in a paycheck which in turn buys groceries and the necessities of life for survival as an earthling.

But we can tune in on the infinite, we can lift our minds to a higher frequency and to a larger Mind than our own, and we can open our hearts to a greater, transcendent Heartbeat through meditation and affirmative thought and prayer. And we can thus change our lives - both on earth and on the Other Side.

This is why you must take time each morning when you are waking and take time every evening in the lateness of the night when you finally are ready for sleep, and take time on several occasions during your busy day - to stop your mind and empty it of all worldly thought - and then through meditation and prayer, open it up the inner thoughts of your Godhead - which are not yours but God's. Or whatever you choose to call the Higher Power within us all that is higher and bigger than ourselves - that magnetic and overwhelming feeling and sense that is more alive than alive and more aware than you have ever known. In these meditation experiences you will begin to perceive the illumination and ineffable, all-knowing, glorious effulgence of God.

Let yourself become electrified and illuminated by this incandescent power that is lying dormant within you. Do this four times a day and your life will be transformed. The light

173

which you generate during these periods of tuning in will continue to radiate throughout the day.

The Godhead within all human beings is the heart and soul of all life itself, not only in your realm but in ours on the Other Side. It is the source of love, compassion, of beauty and grace and is the connection each of us has with the Higher Power, with God and the very creativity of the universe.

Sept. 4:

Your soul contains your true being. Your physical body is but a temporary garment worn during your brief span on earth. You take with you into the next dimension an ethereal body similar in form to your physical body, but much less solid - yet perfect in health, beauty and vitality. You also take with you all the faculties of your presently under-developed senses - sight, hearing, taste, smell and touch - plus your little explored other senses such as ESP (extra-sensory perception) and intuition.

Here in our realm, these other senses - many of them relatively untouched on earth - and many others indescribable in earthling terms - may be utilized and developed and made a part of your psyche and your soul. Your life here is fuller because you are more conscious and the more conscious you are, the more alive you are.

Love, love of another, love of God and love of all God's creatures and of all of God's creation is consciousness at its fullest and the highest form of life and love that we know. The fullness of one's life is determined by the fullness of one's love.

Sept. 13:

The beauty of God's realm on the Other Side is beyond words to describe. If you as an earthling have lived a thoughtful, caring, generous, loving life, you will find yourself in the after-life in a dimension completely in tune with the highest vibrations that have made up your soul. Thus you will feel exalted and inspired and at peace and in harmony in your new surroundings in your new life.

What will you actually be doing? You will commit yourself and your time to becoming totally immersed in the new vibrations that surround you, those which are most akin to your own highest aspirations. This may sound terribly lofty and out-of-this-world but it really is not. It is like going to the finest university and studying and practicing every day the internal development of your higher consciousness. That, too, sounds self-centered and self-seeking on the face of it, but it isn't at all. Because, when you develop the span of your consciousness in length, breadth and depth, you automatically, inevitably, go beyond yourself and become more acutely aware of others, their needs and aspirations. At the same time you are becoming much more conscious of the beauty and glory of the universe and of all God's creatures and creations in it. Not selfishly inward, but outwardly, you grow - in wonder, knowledge and love.

Put specifically and more matter-of-factly, you go to seminars, participate in group discussions, hear lectures and enjoy art, drama and music developing your soul and filling your heart with renewed love and strength. You embark on a rigorous program of spiritual development. But that is only the beginning!

Then, of course, you must utilize your expanded love and understanding and share it with your fellow human beings in the after-life on the Other Side. You will enjoy helping those whose

175

vibrations are not yet at your level who are seeking instructions as to how to achieve higher consciousness through learning exercises and practical experience.

Also, you will help loved ones still on earth to find their way, as you have, to these higher vibrations and new way of life which is so filled with peace, beauty and grace. It is as though you are always on a 'high' - a 'high' of glorious inspiration and love.

The more you study and your consciousness expands, the closer you grow toward the Higher Power and become a part of the Cosmic Consciousness that is the ultimate expression of God's Mind and Heart and Soul and Being.

The ultimate goal is to become one with God, to become so completely a part of God that you are a sheath for God's light, a temple for God's love, and an expression of God's Holy Will in all that you think and say, and do and are!

The source of the automatic writing you have just read will probably remain forever an unanswered mystery. Whether the thoughts came from "guides" or "guardians" from the Other Side - from "the Godhead within us all" - or from what some parapsychologists now call our "super-consciousness" is not really important. What is important is the fact that such well-springs of insight and inspiration are available and can be tapped by all of us through meditation, deep study and prayer.

Regardless of their source, the content of these excerpts reaffirms and amplifies the thrilling testimony regarding life and love beyond death - and for that reason I have included these excerpts here.

Over and over again it is made clear to us that love is the greatest thing in our world - in the next - and in the worlds beyond worlds - into the infinity that makes up God's universe.

Twenty centuries ago, these words were attributed to St. John: *"God is love. Whoever lives in love lives in God and God in him."*[4]

In our own century, less than three decades ago, the Jesuit priest and philosopher, Pierre Teilhard de Chardin wrote in his stirring book, *The Phenomenon of Man* (1959):

> *Love alone is capable of uniting living beings in such a way as to complete and fulfill them by what is deepest in themselves. This is a fact of daily experience. At what moment do lovers come into the most complete possession of themselves if not when they say they are lost in each other?*
>
> *...we should extend our science to its farthest limits and recognize and accept (as being necessary to close and balance space-time) not only some vague future existence, but also, as I must now stress, the radiation as a present reality of that mysterious center of our centers which I have called Omega.*[5]

This is the Omega to which Dr. Kenneth Ring referred in his book, *Heading Toward Omega* when near-death patients felt themselves enveloped and transformed by overwhelming love in the presence of a light or a Being of Light who personified that Love!

Once the presence of that universal love is recognized and embraced in your heart, mind and soul - your happiness will know no bounds. For you will be on your way to becoming one with God's spirit deep within you, one with God's children here and beyond, one with God's world here on earth and one with God's infinite and infinitely beautiful universe!

Then, in truth, it will no longer be you who lives but God lives in you!

177

NOTES AND GENERAL SOURCES

CHAPTER ONE

1. Lawrence LeShan, *The Medium, the Mystic and the Physicist*, New York, Ballantine Books, 1966, pp. 246-247
2. Sherwood Eddy, *You Will Survive After Death*, New York, Rhinehart and Co., 1950, p.7
3. Wilder Penfield, O.M., Litt.B., M.D., F.R.S. *The Mystery of the Mind* - A Critical Study of Consciousness and the Human Brain, Princeton N. J., Princeton University Press, 1975, P. 47
4. ibid., Foreward p.xvii-xviii
5. ibid., p.46
6. ibid., p.61
7. William James, *The Will to Believe and Human Immortality*, New York, Dover, 1956, pp.17-18
8. Lawrence LeShan, *The Medium, the Mystic and the Physicist*, New York, Ballantine Books, 1966, Preface p.x

Socrates:
   Martin Ebon, *They Knew the Unknown*, New York, World Publishing Co., 1971, pp.1-5
   Sherwood Eddy, *You Will Survive After Death*, New York, Rhinehardt and Co., 1950, pp.19-21
   Encyclopedia Britannica, Volume 20, Chicago, London, Toronto, William Benton Publisher, 1961, pp.915-920, Socrates
   Will Durant, *The Life of Greece, Vol. II, The Story of Civilization*, New York, Simon and Schuster, 1939, pp.452-456

9. Geraldine Cummins, *Mind in Life and Death*, London, The Aquarian Press, 1956, p. 19-20
10. Will Durant, *The Story of Philosophy*, New York, Garden City Publishing Co., 1938, pp.11-19

Lincoln:
11. Nettie Colburn Maynard, *Was Abraham Lincoln a Spiritualist?*, Philadelphia, C. Hartranft Publisher, 1891, pp.64-74
12. David C. Knight, *The ESP Reader*, New York, Grossett and Dunlap, 1969, p.32
13. see note 11, pp.92-93
14. ibid., p.74
15. Carl Sandburg, Abraham Lincoln - *The War Years* Vol.II, New York, Harcourt Brace and Co., p.201
16. ibid. Vol.IV, p. 244-245

Edison:
   Martin Ebon, *They Knew the Unknown*, New York, World Publishing Co., 1971, pp.129-138

17. Thomas A. Edison, *The Diary and Sundry Observations of Thomas Alva Edison*, New York, Philosophical, February, 1948
18. Ralph Harlow, *A Life After Death*, Garden City, N.Y., Doubleday and Company, Inc., 1961, p.27
19. Allen Spraggett, *The Case for Immortality*, New York, New American Library, 1974, pp.103-104
20. Martin Ebon, *They Knew the Unknown*, New York, World Publishing Co., 1971, p.136

Brahms:
21. Arthur M. Abell, *Talks with Great Composers,* Eschwege, West Germany, G. E. Schroeder-Verlag, Publisher, 1964, p.11, pp.16-18, 20-29

Handel:
22. *Music of the World's Great Composers, Pleasantville, N.Y., Readers Digest, 1959, p.4*

Maimonides:
23. Volume II *Encyclopedia, Judaica,* New York, The Macmillan Company, 1971, pp.754-781, Maimonides, Moses
24. Louis Jacobs, *What Does Judaism Say About...?* New York, Quadrangle/N.Y. Times Book Co., p.159
25. ibid. p.161

Kant:
26. Volume 13, *Encyclopedia Britannica,* Chicago, London, Toronto, William Benton Publisher, 1961, pp. 266-272
Will Durant, *The Story of Philosophy,* New York, Garden City Publishing Co., Inc., 1938, pp.276-317

Air Chief Marshall Lord Dowding:
Robert Wright, *Dowding and the Battle of Britain,* London, Macdonald and Company, 1969
Air Chief Marshall Lord Dowding, *Many Mansions,* 1943, *Lychgate,* 1945, London, Rider and Co., *The Dark Star,* London, Museum Press Ltd., 1951
Obituary of Lord Dowding, New York Times, Feb. 16, 1970, p.37
27. Air Chief Marshall Lord Dowding, *God's Magic - An Aspect of Spiritualism,* London, The Spiritualist Press, 1948

Moses:
The Books of Exodus, Leviticus, Numbers, Deuteronomy: *The Old Testament*
Volume 15, *Encyclopedia Britannica,* Chicago, London, Toronto, William Benton Publisher, 1961, p.839: Moses
Moshe Pearlman, *In the Footsteps of Moses,* Tel-Aviv, Israel, Leon Amile Publisher, 1973
LaMar C. Berritt, *Discovering the World of the Bible,* Nashville, Tenn.,
Thomas Nelson Publisher, 1979
Mortimer J. Cohen, *Pathways Through the Bible,* Philadelphia, The Jewish Publication Society of America, 1946

Jesus:
The Gospels According to St. Matthew, St. Mark, St. Luke, St. John: *The New Testament*
Will Durant, *Caesar and Christ, Vol. III The Story of Civilization,* New York, Simon and Schuster, 1944, pp.553-574: Chapter xxvi Jesus 4 B.C.- A.D. 30
LaMar Berritt, *Discovering the World of the Bible,* Nashville, Tenn., Thomas Nelson Publisher, 1979

28. Gospel According to St. Matthew: *New Testament,* 5:17
29. Gospel According to St. John: *New Testament,* 14:10
30. ibid., 14:12
31. see note above, Jesus: Will Durant, p. 557

CHAPTER TWO

Lodge:
W. P. Jolly, *Sir Oliver Lodge,* Rutherford-Madison-Teaneck, N.J. Fairleigh Dickinson University Press, 1975
Sir Oliver Lodge, *Raymond or Life and Death,* New York, George H. Doran Company, 1916
Sir Oliver Lodge, *Past Years, - An Autobiography,* New York, Charles Scribner's Sons, 1932
Sir Oliver Lodge, *Raymond Revised - A New and Abbreviated Edition of "Raymond or Life and Death"* with an additional chapter, London, Methuen and Co., Ltd., 1922
Obituary of Sir Oliver Lodge *New York Times,* August 23, 1940. p.15
1. W. P. Jolly, *Sir Oliver Lodge,* Rutherford-Teaneck N.J., Fairleigh Dickinson University Press, 1975, p.186
2. Renée Haynes, *The Society for Psychical Research, 1882-1982; A History,* London, Macdonald, 1982, p.23
3. Sir Oliver Lodge, *Raymond or Life and Death,* New York, George H. Doran Company, 1916, pp.117-120, background on Mrs. Katherine Kennedy.
4. Nandor Fodor, *An Encyclopedia of Psychic Science,* Secaucus, N.J. The Citadel Press, 1966, p. 281: Alfred Vout Peters
John G. Fuller, *The Airmen Who Would Not Die,* New York, G. P. Putnam's Sons, 1979 pp. 72-73: Alfred Vout Peters
5. Suzy Smith, *The Mediumship of Mrs. Leonard,* New Hyde Park, N.Y. University Books, 1964
Nandor Fodor, *An Encyclopedia of Psychic Science,* Secaucus, N.J. The Citadel Press, 1966, pp. 193-195: Mrs. Gladys Osborne Leonard
Rosalind Heywood, *Beyond the Reach of Sense - An Inquiry Into Extra-Sensory Perception,* New York, E. P. Dutton and Co., Inc., 1974, pp. 112-120 Chapter XII - Mediumship-Mrs. Leonard (1) pp. 121-126: Chapter XII - Mediumship-Mrs. Leonard (2)
Gladys Osborne Leonard, *My Life in Two Worlds,* London, Cassell and Co., Ltd., 1942
Biographical Dictionary of Parapsychology, New York, Helix Press-Garrett Publications, 1964, pp. 186-187: Mrs. Gladys Osborne Leonard

CHAPTER THREE

Doyle:
Pierre Nordon, *Conan Doyle - A Biography,* New York, Chicago, San Francisco, Holt, Rhinehart and Winston, 1967
The Rev. John Lamond, D.D., *Arthur Conan Doyle - A Memoir,* London, John Murray, 1931
Arthur Conan Doyle, *Memories and Adventures,* Boston, Little, Brown and Company, 1924
Volume 7, *Encyclopedia Britannica,* Chicago, London, Toronto, William Benton Publisher, 1961, p. 565: Arthur Conan Doyle
Nandor Fodor, *Encyclopedia of Psychic Science,* Secaucus, N.J. The Citadel Press, 1966, pp. 105-107: Sir Arthur Conan Doyle
Obituary *The New York Times* July 8, 1930, p.1, p.4
1. Arthur Conan Doyle, *The New Revelation,* New York, George H. Doran Company, 1918, pp. 31-32
2. Volume 23, *Encyclopedia Britannica,* Chicago, London, Toronto, William Benton Publisher, 1961, p.793Q
3. Colin Wilson, *Afterlife - An Investigation of the Evidence for Life After Death,* Garden City, N.Y., Doubleday and Co., 1987, p.205
4. John Dickson Carr, *The Life of Sir Arthur Conan Doyle,* New York, Harper and Brothers, 1949, p.268
5. ibid. pp.258-259
6. Arthur Conan Doyle, *The Vital Message,* New York, George H. Doran Co. 1919, pp.91-103

CHAPTER FOUR

Terhune:
Anice-Terhune, *The Bert Terhune I Knew,* New York, Harper and Brothers, 1943
Albert Payson Terhune and Anice Terhune, *Across the Line,* New York, E. P. Dutton and Co, Inc., 1945
Obituary of Mrs. Albert Payson Terhune, *New York Times,* Nov. 9, 1964, p.47
1. Volume 21 *Encyclopedia Britannica,* Chicago, London, Toronto, William Benton Publisher, 1961 p.948: Albert Payson Terhune
2. The New Testament
3. Gina Cerminara, *Many Mansions - the Edgar Cayce Story on Reincarnation,* New York, New American Library, 1950, pp.42-43

CHAPTER FIVE

Hinchliffe:
Emilie Hinchliffe, *The Return of Captain W. G. R. Hinchliffe, D.F.C.,A.F.C.,* London, The Psychic Press, 1930
John G. Fuller, *The Airmen Who Would Not Die,* New York, G.P.Putnam's Sons, 1979
1. Frederick Lewis Allen, *Only Yesterday, New York, Harper and Brothers, 1931, pp.216-224*
Volume 4, *Encyclopedia Britannica,* Chicago, London, Toronto, William Benton Publisher, 1961, p.476 : Richard Evelyn Byrd
2. Stoker Hunt, *Ouija - The Most Dangerous Game,* Harper and Row, 1985, pp.3-6, pp. 147-148

Garrett:
Eileen J. Garrett, *My Life As a Search for the Meaning of Mediumship,* London, Rider, 1939
Eileen J. Garrett, *Adventures in the Supernormal,* New York, Creative Age Press, 1949
Eileen J. Garrett, *Many Voices - The Autobiography of a Medium,* New York, G.P.Putnam's Sons, 1968
Obituary, *New York Times,* September 17, 1970
Allan Angoff, *Eileen Garrett and the World Beyond the Senses,* New York, William Morrow and Company, 1974
3. Allan Angoff, *Eileen Garrett and the World Beyond the Senses,* New York, William Morrow and Company, 1974, p. x Introduction
4. Eileen J. Garrett, *Many Voices - TheAutobiography of a Medium,* New York, G.P.Putnam's Sons, 1968, pp.8-9 Introduction by Allan Angoff
5. Emilie Hinchliffe, *The Return of Captain W. G. R. Hinchliffe D.F.C., A.F.C.,* London, The Psychic Press, 1930, pp.69-81

CHAPTER SIX

Moody:
Raymond A. Moody, Jr., M.D., *Life After Life,* New York, Bantam Books, 1975
Reflections on Life After Life, New York, Bantam Books, 1978
with Paul Perry, *The Light Beyond,* New York, Bantam Books, 1988

Ring:
Kenneth Ring, Ph.D., *Life at Death,* New York, Quill, 1982
Heading Toward Omega, New York, William Morrow and Company, 1984

Michael B. Sabom, M.D., F.A.C.C., *Recollections of Death,* A Medical Investigation, New York, Harper and Row, 1982

1. For the full story of Dr. Ritchie's experience as he personally perceived it, read, *Return from Tomorrow* by George G. Ritchie, M.D. with Elizabeth Sherrill, Old Tappan, N.J., Fleming H. Revell Co., 1978.
2. Raymond A. Moody Jr., M.D., *Life After Life,* New York, Bantam Books, 1975
3. George Gallup, Jr. with William Proctor, *Adventures in Immortality,* New York, McGraw-Hill Book Company, 1982, p.17
4. Raymond A. Moody, Jr., M.D., *Life After Life,* pp.31-32
5. ibid., pp.55-66
6. ibid., p.63
7. ibid., pp.65-68
8. ibid., p.90
9. ibid., p.107
10. ibid., p.93
11. ibid., p.94
12. Raymond A. Moody, Jr., M.D., *Reflections on Life After Life,* New York, Bantam Books, 1977, pp.55-62
13. ibid., pp.106-107
14. ibid., p.111
15. ibid., pp.106-107
16. *Psychology Today*, Sept. 1988, article: "Brushes With Death - The evidence from near-death experiences points to a hereafter" by Paul Perry, p.14.
17. Raymond A. Moody, Jr., M.D., *Life After Life,* p.183.
18. ibid., p.183
19. ibid., p.184
20. *U.S.News and World Report* June 11, 1984, Article; "The Near-Death Experience - How Thousands Describe It," An Interview with Dr. Kenneth Ring, p.59
    Also: *Reader's Digest* Aug. 1981, article: "Life After Death: The Growing Evidence" by Mary Ann O'Roark, pp. 52-53
21. see note 20 *U.S.News and World Report*, p.59
22. ibid., p.59
23. *Reader's Digest* Aug. 1981; article: "Life After Death; The Growing Evidence" by Mary Ann O'Roark, p.53
24. ibid., p.52
25. ibid., p.53
26. *U.S.NEWS AND WORLD REPORT,* June 11, 1984, article: "The Near-Death Experience - How Thousands Describe It," an interview with Dr. Kenneth Ring, pp.59-60
27. ibid., p.59
28. see note 23
29. Kenneth Ring, Ph.D., *Life at Death* - A Scientific Investigation of the Near-Death Experience, New York, Quill, 1982, p.264
30. Raymond A. Moody Jr. M.D., *The Light Beyond,* New York, Bantam Books, 1988, pp.121-122
31. see note 29, quotation from back-cover of paperback edition
32. Kenneth Ring Ph.D., *Heading Toward Omega,* Foreward by Dr. Elizabeth Kubler-Ross, p.12
33. ibid., p.100
34. ibid., p.99
35. ibid., p.103
36. ibid., p.109
37. ibid., p.127
38. ibid., p.127
39. ibid., p.128

40. *The Light Beyond,* see note 30, p.110
41. Mary Ann O'Roark, see note 23, p.54
42. *The Light Beyond,* see note 30, p.109
43. Michael B. Sabom, M.D., F.A.C.C., *Recollections of Death: A Medical Investigation,* New York, Harper and Row, 1982, p.133
44. Helen Dukas and Banesh Hoffman, eds., *A. Einstein-The Human Side,* Princeton University Press, 1979, p.33
45. see note 43, p.186
46. Mary Ann O'Roark, see note 23, p.55
47. *The Light Beyond,* see note 30, pp.107-108
48. Mary Ann O'Roark, see note 23, p.55
49. *Life After Life,* p.44
50. *The Light Beyond,* p.77
51. *Life After Life,* p.44
52. *The Light Beyond,* p.83
53. ibid., p.83
54. ibid., p.154
55. ibid., p.155
56. Louis Jacobs, *What Does Judaism Say About -?,* New York, Quadrangle N.Y.Times Books, 1958, p.159

CHAPTER SEVEN

1. Psalm 23:4 *Old Testament*; King James Version
2. Robert H. Ashby, *The Guidebook for the Study of Psychical Research,* New York, Samuel Weiser, Inc., 1972, p.69
3. Frederic W. H. Myers through Geraldine Cummins, *The Road to Immortality,* London, Ivor Nicholson and Watson, 1932, p.20
4. I John 4:16 *New Testament:* New International Version, New York, International Bible Society.
5. Pierre Teilhard de Chardin, *The Phenomenon of Man,* New York, Harper Colophon Books, Harper and Row, 1975, p.265-268

About the Author

In 1978, Dr. David Hyatt was awarded an Honorary Doctor of Laws degree by Sacred Heart University:

- for his zealous commitment to strengthening national unity by fighting bigotry and injustice through dialogue and education...
- for his efforts to sensitize the American community to the destructiveness of prejudice...
- for his impassioned stand against violence and terrorism, poverty and discrimination...
- and for his dynamic leadership in seeking to unify the many diverse peoples of the world.

For nearly three decades Dr. Hyatt served as a professional staff member of an organization dedicated to building interreligious, interracial and intercultural understanding within the U.S. and beyond its boundaries - the National Conference of Christians and Jews. As its president for the nine years until his retirement in 1982, Dr. Hyatt headed the growing and expanding nationwide educational organization with over 70 regional offices and an annual budget which increased from $4 million to $8.5 million raised from corporate and individual gifts. These funds were invested in national and community conferences, institutes, workshops and dialogues involving youth, teachers, parents, police, clergy and business, political, labor, religious and civic leaders throughout the U.S. Since its inception the program has been praised by every incumbent U.S. president for its important contribution to national unity.

Among the program benchmarks under his leadership were:

- a national program in behalf of quality, integrated education in the public schools with Ford Foundation and U.S. government H.E.W. funding,
- a tripling of interracial, interreligious programs for high school youth,
- a nationwide campaign to counter the anti-Semitism and racist actions of increasingly vocal and militant KKK and neo-Nazi groups.
- a series of intercultural seminar tours of Israel, Jordan and Egypt on Christian, Jewish, Moslem relations in the Middle East and programs throughout the U.S. concerning Israel's right to exist in peace and security in the Middle East.
- A nationwide series of annual institutes and conferences on the Holocaust ultimately leading to the establishment of National Holocaust Remembrance Week by Act of Congress.

During this same period Dr. Hyatt was also involved with many other organizations in a leadership or coalition role. He was vice-president and member of the Board of Trustees of the Catholic Interracial Council. He was a founding sponsor of the National Interreligious Task Force for Soviet Jewry and a member of the National Executive board of the America-Israel Friendship League. Among the many related offices he held include, chairman of the Committee on Human Rights for UNESCO, by appointment of Secretary of State, Dean Rusk.

In 1978 Dr. Hyatt was elected president of the International Council of Christians and Jews by delegates from 15 member nations at its annual meeting in Vienna and in 1980 at Sigtuna, Sweden was reelected by acclamation for a second term.

On Dr. Hyatt's "retirement" from the NCCJ in late 1982, President Emeritus Thomas P. Melady, of Sacred Heart University, now American ambassador to the Holy See, Rome, Italy, said of him, "...David is the personification of Teilhard de Chardin's universal man who 'builds the earth.' He has been an architect, a builder, a reconciler. Under his leadership, the NCCJ has entered the world scene." And the late, revered Nathan Perlmutter, the national director of the Anti-Defamation League of B'nai Brith, said: "You, by daring to be forthright, by taking positions on issues which some shunned for fear of being deemed 'controversial,' gave strength to us all..."

Prior to joining the National Conference Dr. Hyatt was associated with the investment brokerage house of Merril Lynch, Pierce, Fenner and Smith and also was manager of public relations for the Hartford Accident and Indemnity Company of the Hartford Insurance Group. From 1948 to 1950 he was on the faculty of Cornell University. He holds a B.A. from Northwestern and an M.A. and doctorate in education from Columbia University.

Prior to the U.S. entry into World War II, outraged and sickened by the barbarism of Hitler and Nazi Germany, particularly for its extermination of the Jews, through the American Field Service he volunteered to serve without pay as an ambulance driver in the British Eighth Army and served for nearly two years from 1941 to 1943 in the North African desert in Egypt and Libya. He was cited for work under fire. From 1943 to 1945 he served as a lieutenant in the U.S. Navy's air arm.

Dr. Hyatt has had a life-long interest in the subject of life after death, prompted in part by his experiences with death and during his service as a frontline ambulance driver during World War II. He is a Fellow of the American Society for Psychical Research and this book is the product of many years of thoughtful, penetrating research and deep, personal reflection.

Most of the facts cited above are more fully described in my biography of my husband, *Bonfires at Heaven's Gate*, (Seabury Press,1983). As Dr. Hyatt's wife and partner for many years, I shared his aspirations and worked closely with him during the fervent years he was president of the NCCJ and during his continuing years of "retirement." I have often spoken of our years together as "a great adventure!" It continues to be so.

Lillian L. Hyatt
July, 1992

Testimonials

"Recovering from cancer surgery and chemotherapy, I faced my own mortality with depression and fear; then reading *Your Life and Love Beyond Death*, each succeeding page touched on a world beyond, lightening my spirit. Now I feel I have tangible proof that I will eventually be reunited with my loved ones in the next dimension. Thanks to Dr. Hyatt's beautiful book, now I know that life goes on beyond death and I have no fear."

Mrs. Esther Whiting, Ft. Lauderdale, Florida

"Dr. Hyatt's rich examples of psychical evidence will gain the respect of both skeptic and believer. An impressive case for immortality and for communication with the dead - and an important contribution to the field!"

Allan Angoff,
author of *Eileen Garrett and the World Beyond the Senses*

"My deepest gratitude for *Your Life and Love Beyond Death*. It's wonderful words of comfort and support during the difficult times since the passing of my dear wife were a great blessing to me. It so strongly reassured me that she still lives and is often with me as I am with her. This book is terrific in every respect - factual, informative, uplifting and inspiring!"

Dr. Sam Brown,
New Jersey Regional Director Emeritus
of the American Jewish Congress

"To those trying to adjust to a life after the loss of a dearly beloved, *Your Life and Love Beyond Death* will be of invaluable help. It was to me... Dr. Hyatt's vivid and fascinating examples of actual experiences, his exciting method of presentation and his earnest belief in the subject all blend to make a heart-moving yet scholarly and credible case for life after death..."

Mrs. Laura Holland, longtime national leader
of the American Red Cross, Bronxville, N.Y.

"I have never worried about heaven because Christ said, 'I go to prepare a place for you.' But since reading your book, the verse 'In my Father's house are many mansions,' now takes on a new meaning for me."

Mrs. Margaret Reynolds, homemaker, mother of five, church leader,
Ashtabula, Ohio

"An astonishing treatise! Here are disclosures of apparent communications from the Other Side documented by distinguished investigators and brought into a single volume from widely varied sources. The author's narration of his own personal psychic experiences will bring tears to your eyes... This is the statement of a brilliant scholar who is definitely a 'believer.' But let the 'unbeliever' be warned: the writing is so exciting and convincing - almost breathless in its pace - *watch yourself* - you just may be swept away!"

Roger B. Bernhardt, Ph.D.,
psychologist - psycho-analyst, New York City

"Thanks a million for sending me your book after Harry's passing. *Your Life and Love Beyond Death* is so true. It was a great help to all of us. Gary, my oldest who as you know is a pilot for Northwest Airlines, said what you described was just what Harry hoped for. And Frank, my second son, says he just knows now that Harry is still with us. Your book gave me strength and gave it to many others too. Bless you for writing and sending it to me."

Mrs. Marion Webb, Safety Harbor, Florida

"Anyone who believes in life after death must read David Hyatt's *Your Life and Love Beyond Death*. It has charm, whimsy and is an enthralling vision of what life may be like after our short span on earth.

"As Dr. Hyatt points out, some of our greatest poets, authors, geniuses of music, philosophers, aviators, scientist and inventors have long had the feeling that there was a life beyond our present one - and Edison, Brahms, Kant, Maimonides, William James, Sir Oliver Lodge, Conan Doyle, RAF Capt. Raymond Hinchliffe, Albert Payson Terhune and many others speak out dramatically in this book, giving us their fascinating insights into our life beyond this life.

"In another chapter you won't be able to put down, he explores the phenomenon and the spiritual mystery of 'the Near-Death-Experience.' Having survived an NDE myself and witnessed the NDE testimony of some of my patients, I can personally corroborate the findings in his exciting presentation.

"Equally absorbing are his own psychic experiences while a soldier in World War II. His personal insights are profoundly challenging and his swift, incisive writing makes for delightful, easy reading. His book gave me a feeling of euphoria, of exaltation when I finished it. Read it. You'll love it! I did."

Robert Blaine, M.D.
internist, New York City

"Unforgettably, under great stress and near death fifteen years ago, I saw the 'white light' and a partial view of what was beyond - several of my relatives who had passed on were waiting for me - I remember pleading that I wasn't ready, I still had things to do... In his book, Dr. Hyatt understands such an experience and has taken the finality out of the word *death* because he knows - as I know from my own unforgettable experience - that there is no ending to our life and love beyond death... He has written a sensitive, wonderful book!"

Julie Small, New York, N.Y.

"As a skeptic, I at first read the book with reluctance and a 'show-me' attitude. But then skepticism seemed to lose ground and credibility started to take over. I found myself captivated by the novelty of the material and by the way the book was written with each story told so warmly and meaningfully...I can't say that I am convinced but I will say that if I ever found a thesis believable, this one put me on the brink."

Mrs. Sylvia Reback
community leader, San Francisco, CA

"As a former reference librarian, writer and editor, I am impressed by the research and scholarship of *Your Life and Love Beyond Death*. It is a work of the highest caliber and I'm sure many other readers will find it as fascinating as I did. Although I was already familiar with the writings of Raymond Moody and other authors cited, Dr. Hyatt gave me many new avenues to explore and fresh insights to ponder. I particularly appreciated his personal psychic experiences and explorations of higher consciousness. Anyone seeking solace for the loss of a loved one - and that includes practically all of us - will find Dr. Hyatt's book a comfort and a blessing!"

Mrs. Mary Lou Tipton
Memphis, Tennessee

"I found the book not only extremely readable but downright fascinating! It makes a very strong case for life after death. I was especially impressed by the array of notables including scientists who support this thesis. It has greatly clarified, as well as reinforced, my personal belief in a hereafter."

Ralph Owen, artist, illustrator,
retired art director of national advertising agency,
Clifton, New Jersey

"As you know, I was brought up, almost from birth, in a Catholic orphanage. Before reading your book I had always looked upon death with great uncertainty and terrible fear. Now a sense of peace has taken over that fear and I have a feeling of joy about where I may be going after my time on earth. Most important of all, I now believe I will one day be reunited with my loved ones and especially my mother and father whom I have never seen. Now I will never feel alone or lonely again.

"I am fascinated by the idea of caring for loved ones on the Other Side and the idea that they are still very much alive and loving and caring for us. And I am excited by being able to clearly envision for the first time what life might be like in the next dimension."

Mrs. Henrietta Alexander, executive secretary
Manchester, Connecticut

"As a clergyman I have stood at the graveside with many a dear family trying to provide comfort and understanding as they parted company with a loved one. Would there be a reunion on the Other Side, and if so, what form would it take?

"My long-time friend, Dr. David Hyatt, wrestles with these inevitable questions in his intriguing book, *Your Life and Love Beyond Death*. Noting the great affirmations of faith in life after death by all of the major living religions of the world, he shares with us many moving, mystical experiences, both personal and as recorded by others, between the living and the socalled 'dead.'

"I share Dr. Hyatt's strong belief in immortality, particularly its influence on life here and now, and I commend his book to anyone searching for an answer to humankind's immortality as well as to everyone who is a believer but would still like to bolster his or her basic faith in life after death."

Dr. Peter Mellette,
Baptist minister, ecumenical leader
Richmond, Virginia

"In *Your Life and Love beyond Death*, David Hyatt has leaped beyond conventional thanatology to give us a fascinating glimpse into spiritualism and more importantly, **spirituality**. His writing is not only engaging, but reveals the author's innate sensitivity and basic love of humanity. Here death has lost its sting, and becomes a subject to be contemplated without fear or trepidation. His thesis is intriguing, as is the documentation he has carefully collected from many notable sources. ...of unusual interest to both scholar and general reader."

Raphael Reider, M.D.
San Francisco, CA

"What a revelation it would be for all of the scholars of the scientific realm to read your book, Dr. Hyatt! Your portrayal of life after death in *Your Life and Love Beyond Death*, using sources of unimpeachable integrity, is so captivating, clear and concise it should impress even the most skeptical. Persons of such impeccable scientific qualifications as Sir Oliver Lodge, Sir Arthur Conan Doyle, Sir William Crooks have long pointed the way for earnest, objective investigation into the mystical realm. The work of Dr. Raymond Moody, Dr. Kenneth Ring and Elizabeth Kubler-Ross also indicated an awakening interest by the scientific minded. ...Your book belongs on the reading list of everyone who is seeking truth and freedom from the errors of age-old ideology and rigid dogma concerning life after death!"

Rev. Donald H. Haddick
Pastor of the Golden Gate Spiritualist Church of San Francisco
President of the California Assoc. of Spiritualist Churches

"The book was a joy to read! The testimony of so many talented and dedicated people gave me a wonderful sense of awareness of what life can be on the Other Side. Dr. Hyatt's personal experiences and conclusions were also engrossing and intriguing to me. I am eagerly looking forward to sharing this book with others. ...it fills a very special longing within us all for an affirmation of the hope of 'life everlasting.' This book is a beautiful testimony to that very great hope!"

Mrs. Vera L. Voigt, Elderhostel Program
San Francisco State University

"What a thought-provoking, stimulating book - not only incredibly well researched and brilliantly organized, but beautifully written and spiritually enlightening! What a refreshing joy it was to read such optimism and faith about our life beyond backed up with convincing evidence to prove it! It should give new hope to many who might otherwise feel despair about 'death.'"

Sally Bingham, San Francisco

"A fascinating book! Any skeptic would and should joyfully acknowledge its convincing proof of life in another dimension. Dr. Hyatt has skillfully and dramatically presented a credible and documented dialogue between eminent individuals and their departed loved ones. And the magnitude of his research should certainly spark impetus for many to personally explore the mystery of 'life and love beyond death.'"

Mrs. Evelyn Kirschenbaum, community leader, Purchase, N.Y.

ACKNOWLEDGEMENTS
Many Prayers Answered

My five children and their spouses became a veritable fan club for the book. For their encouraging support, I am affectionately indebted to: Ellen Cleve Hyatt, Caroline and Peter Parkhurst, Larry and Dianne Richards-Reiss, Ellen M. and Martin J. Silverman and Ann and Geoffrey Hyatt-Smith.

For their personal laudatory endorsements of my initial text, my deep appreciation to three distinguished members of the healing professions and five outstanding clergy leaders - all of them treasured friends: Dr. Roger B. Bernhardt, New York psychologist, psycho-analyst and author; Dr. Robert Blaine, New York internist; Dr. Donald H. Haddick, pastor of the Golden Gate Spiritualist Church of San Francisco; Dr. Peter Mellette, Vice President Emeritus of the National Conference of Christians and Jews; Dr. Raphael Reider, San Francisco cardiologist and our beloved family physician; The Right Rev. John S. Spong, Bishop of the Episcopal Diocese of Newark, N.J.; and Dr. Carl Herman Voss, Protestant minister, ecumenical leader and author.

On an intuitive hunch, I mailed Allen Spraggett, author with William V. Rauscher of *The Man Who Talked With The Dead*, the first copy of my finished text, asking for his reaction. When I phoned him a week later, he replied, "I've just read it cover to cover in one sitting - I couldn't put it down. It will have great appeal. Don't give up on it - it will be published!" I shall forever bless Allen Spraggett for his glowing "green light!"

I sent copies to Dr. Raymond A. Moody, Dr. Kenneth Ring and Dr. Michael B. Sabom to check for accuracy my account of their pioneer research substantiating "the near-death experience." Dr. Ring and Dr. Sabom immediately approved my writing concerning their work, and Dr. Ring generously expressed admiration for the tenor of the book. When I could not reach Dr. Moody by mail or phone over a four month period due to his illness, Dr. Stanley Krippner, vice-president of the American Society for Psychical Research and Director of the Center for Consciousness Studies at the Saybrook Institute in San Francisco, helpfully located him for me. Dr. Moody, now on the faculty of the West Georgia State College, enthusiastically endorsed the text and recommended John White as a possible literary agent, a crucial step in my book's publication. To these four esteemed scholars I am also indebted for their inestimable assistance.

I want to acknowledge the help of the splendid libraries of the American Society for Psychical Research, the Parapsychology Foundation, the University of San Francisco, San Francisco State University, and the fantastic work of the Inter-Library Loan System which enabled me to have access to invaluable, out-of-print volumes.

I want to particularly thank James G. Matlock for his splendid assistance while he was Librarian for the American Society for Psychical Research in checking the accuracy of many historical details. I also want to thank A.S.P.R.'s current librarian John La Martine for his invaluable assistance. In addition I am indebted to Wayne Norman, who while librarian of the Parapsychology Foundation opened up the Foundation's extensive library resources to me, and for also asking Mrs. Eileen Colby, the president of the Foundation, to check for the accuracy of the chapter dealing with her mother, the great psychic medium Eileen Garrett. Mrs. Colby graciously commented that those grieving the loss of a loved one, "will welcome the wealth of information in this book."

I also want to express my deep gratitude to over fifty dear friends and other thoughtful and generous people who previewed my manuscript over the past three years and offered not only their encouragement but their personal testimonials. This diverse group of people from all walks of life whose one common denominator was our friendship, found the text in some cases to be "enthralling," "uplifting," and to a few of them who had suffered the loss of a beloved "a great solace," "a source of new hope," and "an invaluable help to me."

These valued people listed with my warmest thanks are: Henrietta Alexander, Theresa Alexander, Martha and Leonard Aries, Gregory Bernhardt, Sally Bingham, Doris Blaine, Dr. Sam Brown, Arthur Colton, Dora and Robert Cox, Katherine Dietzel Cox, Paige Satorious Dietz, Kitty and Bud Ebbert, Donald Fassett, Georgean Heller, Laura Holland, Hudson Hyatt, Dr. Rex Hutchins, Robert Jones, Evelyn and Henry Kirchenbaum, Frances Lana, Sheila and Jacinto Marrero, Dr. Susan Mellette, Lilli and Ralph Owen, Sylvia Reback, Freda Reider, Gerald Renner, Margaret Reynolds, Manny and Ruth Rosen, Julia Small, Terry Sellard, Dr. Robert W. Siebenschuh, Janet and Richard Smith, Jeffrey Spence, Charlotte Teller, Mary Lou and William H. Tipton, Peggy Tom, Victoria Trostel, Arlene Tucker, Marion Webb and the wonderful Webb family, Esther and Russell Whiting and Gerhard Winkler.

Alfred Lord Tennyson once wrote,"More things are wrought by prayer than this world dreams of." It seems clear to me that this book didn't just happen. Over a hundred extraordinary people were involved in its development. God bless each and every one of you for your valuable help!